Ἡμερολόγιο

ΒΗΡΥΤΟΣ (Ι)

1.1.53
~~28 Δεκ. 52~~ — 15 Αυγ. 54.

κύριως(a): 6.11.53 - 9.12.53 : 6ιχ. 22-59

Γιώργος Σεφέρης

Μετά σελ 83: "Κυπριακά —

(83 φύλλα)

A LEVANT JOURNAL

11 Σεπ. '41.

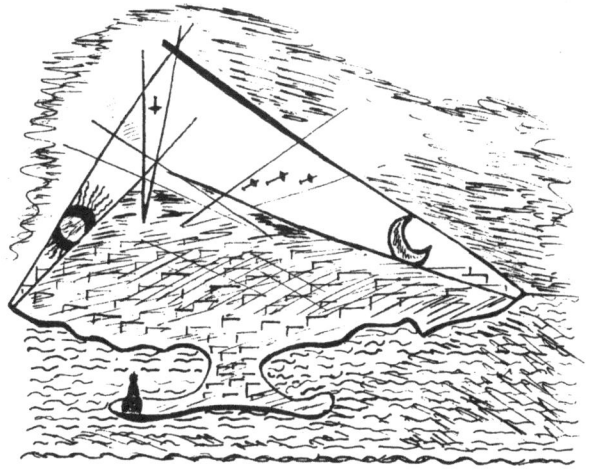

GEORGE SEFERIS

A LEVANT JOURNAL

Translated, Edited, and Introduced by
Roderick Beaton

A Levant Journal, by George Seferis, introduction, translation, and annotation copyright © 2007 Ibis Editions and Roderick Beaton
Greek text of poems and diaries copyright © Anna Londou

All rights reserved. Except brief passages in a newspaper, magazine, radio, or television review, no part of this book may be reproduced in any form or by any means, electronic or mechanical, including photocopying and recording or by any information storage or retrieval system, without permission in writing from the publisher.

Original Greek publication:
Meres 4 (Athens: Ikaros, 1977)
Meres 6, ed. Panagiotis Mermigkas (Athens: Ikaros, 1986)
Poiemata, 8th ed. (Athens: Ikaros, 1972)

The publication of this book was made possible by a generous grant from the Greek Foreign Ministry and the Hellenic-American Chamber of Commerce.

Special thanks are due to Deputy Foreign Minister Theodoros Kassimis, as well as to Catherine Boura, Consul General of Greece in New York, for her ongoing support of this project. Thanks, too, to Stamatis Gikas.

The publisher and translator wish to express their gratitude to Anna Londou, for giving her blessing to this book.

Additional thanks go to Edmund Keeley and the Princeton University Library, Rare Books Division, Department of Rare Books and Special Collections, for permission to reproduce the drawings from *Logbook II*.

Book design: Assia Vilenkin, S&R Design, Jerusalem

10 9 8 7 6 5 4 3 2 1

ISBN 965-90125-6-X

Ibis Editions
POB 8074
German Colony
Jerusalem
Israel
www.ibiseditions.com

CONTENTS

Translator's Introduction   *xiii*

A Levant Journal
   Part I: Wartime (1941–1944)   3
   Part II: The Passing of Empire (1953–1956)   99

Notes   153

Photos and Illustrations   171

TRANSLATOR'S INTRODUCTION

George Seferis was known during his lifetime (1900-1971) chiefly as a poet in the spare, densely allusive modernist manner of T.S. Eliot, and also as a remarkable essayist on literary and cultural topics. Since his death, further aspects of this fascinating literary personality have come to light, with the successive publication of a novel, several collections of personal letters, and, to date, nine volumes of a journal that will eventually span almost the whole of the poet's life, beginning in 1916 and ending on the eve of his death. It is all the more surprising, then, that relatively little attention has yet been devoted to Seferis as a diarist, with only a single volume from his diaries available before now in English translation.*

While he was serving at the Greek Embassy in Ankara, Turkey, in 1948, Seferis first began arranging and editing the scattered journals he had been keeping over the years. More systematically, in the late 1960s, he began to edit some of them into volumes that were clearly intended for publication, giving them the title *Meres*, meaning "Days," probably alluding to the Alexandrian Greek poet C.P. Cavafy (1863–1933), several of whose poems have titles in the form "Days of 1903," "Days of 1896." It is not certain whether any of these volumes of *Days* might have been intended by Seferis to appear while he was alive. His editorial work on them was interrupted by the *coup d'état* of April 21, 1967, which marked the beginning of a period of military rule in his country that would last beyond the poet's death, until 1974. Like many other Greek writers of stature, Seferis made a principled decision not to publish under the harsh regime of censorship imposed by the "Colonels," as Greece's new rulers came to be known. When Seferis died in September 1971, the project had not advanced, and he would become known as a diarist only posthumously.

In the case of Seferis, it is debatable whether one should speak of a single "journal" or a series of different "journals." In his notebooks he himself made a clear distinction between the personal journal(s), the *Days*, and what he called his "Service Journal," of which two volumes have appeared in Greek under the title *Political Diary*. These deal essentially with matters pertaining to Seferis's lifelong career as a civil servant in the Greek Ministry of Foreign Affairs, in which he eventually rose to the rank of ambassador. The evidence of Seferis's personal archive, preserved in the Gennadius Library,

Athens, is inconclusive as to how consistently he maintained this distinction in practice. Leaving aside the somewhat special case of the *Political Diary*, there are many gradations of difference even within the *Days*. The volume covering the 1920s, for instance, is highly literary and self-conscious in style, almost totally devoid of factual or personal information; the one that covers the early 1930s has been culled from a series of intimate letters. It is only from the mid-1930s onwards that the *Days* settle down, more or less, to the sharply drawn sketches and more relaxed meditations that many readers of these volumes in Greek have admired. But even here, the density and type of entry vary greatly, as does the extent of later reworking. Finally, the balance of introspection, observation, political and cultural commentary shifts from period to period, sometimes even within a single volume. As a result, even if one were to speak of a single journal, the *Days*, that would not be to imply a homogeneous, continuous testimony.

The entries translated here have been selected from two periods in the poet's life when for historical and professional reasons he was stationed in the Levant, a term I use broadly to indicate the eastern rim of the Mediterranean, its hinterland, and the ambit of its historical culture. The first period, represented by the section to which I have given the title "Wartime (1941–1944)," covers the years when Seferis served the Greek government-in-exile in Egypt, during most of World War II, with a brief sojourn in what was then British-mandated Palestine. The second records the experiences of the poet-diplomat while he was based in Beirut, as ambassador simultaneously to Lebanon, Syria, Jordan, and Iraq in the 1950s; during this time he also travelled in a private capacity to Cyprus.

The translated entries amount to perhaps a little over half the material originally published in Greek. Coverage, as is generally the case throughout the later volumes of Seferis's diaries, is highly variable. The narrative of a single day in 1956, during which the poet was diverted by air from Baghdad to Tehran because of a dust-storm, occupies almost six pages in the original diary (and here is given in full); conversely, the first four months of 1944, one of the most momentous periods in the history of the wartime Greek government-in-exile which Seferis served, are represented by only ten. In the latter case, the omission is made good in the *Political Diary*. Sometimes, also, sheer pressure of work seems to have been a constraint. This might be the reason for the scarcity of entries during the second half of 1943, for example. And it is evident that not everything that might have been of interest to his readers today caught Seferis's attention in the same way. The entry for Saturday, August 7, 1943, might be taken as indicative of how certain impressions may have "functioned" for Seferis the diarist, as well as for the poet, while others did not.

I have chosen in this selection to highlight the poet's engagement with the civilizations through which he passed, and with the legacy of their ancient and more recent past. I have also included everything that relates to his own work as a poet and the creative process as it is reflected in the diaries. Conversely, I have omitted a large amount of material that deals more or less exclusively with the Greek politics in which Seferis was deeply involved at this time, or with events in Greece about which he learned on his travels. One rule of thumb governing the selection has been a desire to keep the amount of annotation to a minimum; another has been the wish to bring out the underlying coherence of Seferis's portrait of the region—something which, it must be remembered, was never intended by the author of these pages himself. I would like to think that the *Levant Journal* can be read as a piecemeal record of one man's engagement with those lands and the people he met there.

Seferis possessed very powerfully the faculty termed by T.S. Eliot the "historical sense." The records left by Seferis in this journal of his travels in the Levant are just as much records of particular *moments* in the troubled history of the region as they are of the places through which he passed. Seferis's Egypt is not the "eternal" Egypt of the pyramids (which he barely mentions) or even of the Nile (though he did write a poem about it): it is the Egypt of Shepheard's (now vanished) Hotel; of displaced, disgruntled, and scheming politicians; of a nominally neutral, sovereign country, in which everything is high-handedly controlled from the British Embassy with its watered lawns, but where Arab taxi drivers avoid the main streets for fear of drunken British soldiers throwing beer bottles. In the same way, Jerusalem—as Seferis experienced it during the sudden "Flap" (a polite word in the English of the period, denoting collective panic) when it seemed, in the summer of 1942, that Egypt, too, might fall to the Nazis—was not so much the holy place of three great religions but the ultimate refugee camp.

Similarly, when he came to travel through the Middle East and Cyprus in the 1950s, there is an overarching political context that determines much that Seferis sees and records there. Wherever he went in Lebanon, Syria, Jordan, and Iraq, the ruins of ancient theaters and public buildings reminded him of a great empire—a Greek one, founded by Alexander the Great—that had long ago become a "spent power." This phrase would recur in the poem he wrote about Cyprus, "Engomi," included here. But as he travelled through the newly independent Arab states of the Middle East, Seferis was acutely aware of how heavily lay the recent legacy of Western rule; he was not encouraged by signs that its place was rapidly being taken by American consumerism. At least in the countries where he was serving professionally as a diplomat, the last shackles of imperial control had overtly been cast off. The same was not so of Cyprus, which Seferis now visited for the first time.

In Cyprus, Seferis found "a world of people speaking Greek, a Greek world,"* indeed one that reminded him powerfully of the world he had known as a young boy in the seaside villages near his native Smyrna. But even as Seferis visited, the battle-lines were being drawn for one of the last, drawn-out conflicts that would mark the end of the British Empire. The British government, first under Eden, then under Macmillan, seemed determined to flex its muscles and not yield to growing pressure from the Greek Orthodox Christians of Cyprus for union (*Enosis*) with Greece. Seferis saw beyond the partisan struggle that was then developing and recognized what would turn out to be the true, underlying historical dynamic of these events: another great empire was at this very moment following in the footsteps of the one founded by Alexander the Great towards dissolution, and it was madness on the part of the British government—and of many of Seferis's British friends who supported it—to pretend otherwise. The title I have added to Part II, "The Passing of Empire (1953-1956)," is intended to encapsulate both that historical process, as Seferis observed it on his travels, and his own individual, thoughtful response to what he observed.

But the "historical sense," for Seferis, was acutely attuned not only to the countries that he visited. Wherever he went, he carried with him a deep sense of his own country's long and often traumatic history. "Travel wherever I might, it is Greece that causes me pain," he had written in a poem back in 1936. This often-quoted line could well serve as an epigraph for Seferis's diaries of the Levant. Displaced to Egypt by the Nazi invasion of Greece in April 1941, Seferis could never forget the circumstances that had forced him from his home, or his terrible anxiety for the country he had left behind, undergoing the hardships of a brutal occupation. And in the 1950s, as he experienced the bumpy transition towards a post-colonial Middle East, his comparison between the situation of the Greeks of Cyprus and the Arabs of the neighboring lands lends a spur to all that he sees and to much of his commentary on it.

As a diarist, scarcely less than as a poet, Seferis bears powerful witness to the crises of the age in which he lived. But he does not pretend to be a fully impartial observer. Reading Seferis, we are frequently and insistently reminded that this particular witness hails from a particular part of the globe and has been brought up on a particular digest of European civilization as it was understood in the early part of his century, a civilization whose development can be traced back in all its stages to its origins in the pre-classical world of ancient Greece.

From the perspective of the early twenty-first century, it is as much as anything Seferis's own cultural baggage, which he brings to the places he visits, that makes for the interest of these journals. True, since the decades when he was there, the places he records have for the most part changed, sometimes beyond recognition. Details of British-administered Palestine before 1947, of East Jerusalem when it belonged to Jordan, of Iraq under Nuri Said, of Cyprus on the eve of the violent anti-colonial conflict of the late 1950s—all these are vivid reminders of worlds that no longer exist, but which crucially shaped the one that we live in today. But in all that he records, Seferis observes *as a Greek*.

This perspective gives a new twist to the inevitable "orientalism" that many readers will detect in these diaries. It is all too familiar to read, in the travel-writing of Europeans, that Arabs are noisy and observe poor public hygiene, or that the spread of Coca-Cola and other symptoms of American consumerism have a corrupting effect upon traditional societies. But Seferis knows that many of these charges are at the same time being levelled by western Europeans against his own fellow-Greeks; the unthinking colonial snobbism towards "Arabs" (Seferis hardly ever, for instance, refers to "Egyptians") that he sees around him, and sometimes criticizes, is part of his own European upbringing too; he cannot help but perpetuate it. At one point, on his first visit to Jerusalem in 1942, Seferis reflects explicitly on the perpetually ambiguous situation of the Greek, caught midway between East and West. A further nuance derives from the fact that Seferis's own family came from the eastern seaboard of the Aegean, from what is now Turkey. Displaced to Greece by the Greek-Turkish war of 1919-1922, Greeks like Seferis would be stigmatized for more than a generation afterwards as "Levantines." For all the depth of his European culture, Seferis, too, had once been at home in the Levant, and he never allows himself to forget it.

A running theme throughout this journal is that of "exile." Seferis for much of his life considered himself as doubly an exile: he had been displaced from his native Smyrna to Athens at an early age and then, as a diplomat, spent the greater part of his professional life far from the country in which he had made his home. If this "Levant journal" in part resembles Western travel literature—and, as is evident from these pages, Seferis himself was certainly very well read in that literature—it has one significant difference: just like Odysseus, the legendary hero for whom he had a lifelong admiration, Seferis was a most reluctant traveller. For Seferis, as for Homer's wanderer and for very many other Greeks in between, travel is not a luxury to be enjoyed; its goal is not "to seek, to find, and not to yield," as Tennyson's poem "Ulysses" has it, but simply: to return to the place where one is at home. Homer's Odysseus longs for his *nostimon hemar* (day of returning), an expression that gives us our modern word *nostalgia*.Seferis, for all the acuteness of his observation and the constant liveliness of his reflections on everything that he sees, shares this longing. "Exile," in Seferis's vocabulary, referring to the experience of displacement, is a more painful and more complex thing than what many Westerners over the centuries have come to call "travel," or its modern descendant, "tourism." Seferis's impressions of his travels in the Levant, then, are at the same time also the record of that sense of *dis*-placement, of being forcibly separated from a place and from people with whom one experiences a sense of organic affinity.

Along with selections from the *Meres* (*Days*), I have included translations of five poems from *Logbook II* (1944), and one from *Logbook III* (1955), though it should be stressed that the finished poems do not appear in the journals themselves. Often, entries in the diary function as silent commentary, elucidation, or even as working drafts of the finished poems. Conversely, each of these poems encapsulates something of the broader and deeper experience drawn by Seferis out of the day-to-day particularities of his travels, some of which have been caught and fixed, in the manner of photographs, in entries in his journal. One should not, of course, read a poem as though it were a diary entry or vice versa, and I hope that the juxtaposition points up the differences between the two kinds of writing, even (or perhaps especially) when the raw material appears to be the same.

This is particularly true, for example, of the poems "Stratis Thalassinos at the Dead Sea" and "Engomi," in which whole phrases, and specific details, can be matched respectively in the diary entries for July 24, 1942, and for the two dates in 1953 and 1954 when Seferis visited the archaeological site of Engomi, near the east coast of Cyprus. In other poems, it can be seen that the particular experience recorded in the diaries has been assimilated over a longer period. "Days of June '41," for instance, despite its dateline, was actually written some months later, in September; by that time Seferis could look back on the events of June 1941 from the greater distance of South Africa, where he had been sent in the meantime. The same can be said of "Last Stop," written in southern Italy on the eve of Seferis's longed-for return to Greece, as World War II was ending; in densely powerful imagery, that poem sums up much of the accumulated feelings, perceptions, and sorrow over the human condition that had been building in Seferis during his three and a half years of exile.

Throughout the excerpts that follow, closed ellipses […] indicate that part of the entry has been omitted by the editor. Open ellipses [. . .] replicate Seferis's. Information on the context of the journal entries can be found in the introductions that precede each of the book's two main sections. More specific matters are explained by endnotes to the entries themselves. (Glossed items are indicated by an asterisk.) In many minor matters, such as the arrangement of the elements in headings to each entry, spelling of non-Greek words and names, punctuation and capitalization, I have followed the published text in Greek, rather than attempt to standardize them. Sometimes in these entries Seferis writes in the first-person singular, but often in the plural. On all the travels covered here, the poet was accompanied by his wife, Maro, whose name appears quite rarely.

King's College London
January 2007

A LEVANT JOURNAL

PART I

WARTIME (1941–1944)

George Seferiades was born in Izmir/Smyrna, then part of the Ottoman Empire, on February 29, 1900. The name "Seferis" is a literary pseudonym, adopted in 1931, when his first book of poems was published. Like many Greek writers of the twentieth century, Seferis as a young man studied law, in his case in Paris in the early 1920s. Returning to Greece, he entered the service of his country's Ministry of Foreign Affairs in 1926. After several years there, Seferis's diplomatic career, before World War II, took him to London and then to Körçe (Albania). When Greece was invaded by fascist Italy on October 28, 1940, Seferis was the official spokesman of the Greek government for the foreign press. During the winter of 1940–1941, the Greek army pushed back the invaders through the mountains of Albania, a heroic episode in modern Greek history and the only military success against the Axis at this early period in the war. Then in April 1941, Hitler came to the rescue of his ally Mussolini, and Greece was placed under occupation by the Axis powers.

As a senior civil servant, Seferis followed the Greek government into exile, first to Crete (April–May 1941), then to Egypt. A Levant Journal opens with Seferis arriving at Port Said. With him is his wife, Maro, with whom he had been living for several years, but had married only on the eve of their evacuation from Athens.

By this time Seferis had established his reputation in Greece as one of the foremost talents of Greek modernism. He had published five collections of verse and a number of highly regarded essays. His work was still barely known abroad, although the first translations of individual poems, into French and English, were beginning to appear. Ironically enough, it was to be his displacement to Egypt for much of the war that was to bring Seferis into close contact with the English poets and intellectuals who would later help to secure his international reputation. Among these, the best known today is Lawrence Durrell, author of The Alexandria Quartet, and known to Seferis as "Larry." Tantalizingly, almost nothing is said in Seferis's journal for this period about these developing relationships.

After the fall of Crete at the end of May 1941, there remained no part of Greece free of Axis control. The politicians who made up the Greek government-in-exile, and their civil servants, including Seferis, were shunted by the British between Cairo and Alexandria. Soon it was decided that the official seat of the exiled government would be London, although much of its work would continue to be done in Cairo. (Egypt *at this time, nominally an independent, "neutral" country, was in fact governed through the British Embassy in Cairo, which was also home to the Allied military high command for the region during much of the war.)*

Seferis found himself professionally side-lined for a time, acting as deputy in the newly established embassy in South Africa. Then in April 1942, almost a year after he had first arrived there from Crete, he found himself summoned back to Egypt, where for the next two years he served as the Greek government's official press spokesman in Cairo, making frequent visits to Alexandria. The political backbiting and intrigue that surrounded him found its way into his next collection of poems, Logbook II, *which would be published in Alexandria at the end of 1944, just after Seferis and Maro had finally left Egypt to return to Greece. That return was to be delayed by a "last stop," of several weeks, in southern Italy, where the poem of that title was written.*

R.B.

1941

Friday, 16 May

We arrive at Port Said today, so we're told. We must be close. No sign of the coast, but it's been explained to us it lies lower than the surface of the sea.

...

Evening, Port Said, Hotel "Casino"

Egypt, the low-lying land. The lowest-lying I've ever seen. Not a hill on the horizon. The tallest things in sight, as you approach: the ships and the houses. The sea looks yellow: the sea of Proteus, and jelly-fish, a great many jelly-fish, deep blue.

...

I think of Cavafy, as I inspect this low-lying land. His poetry is like that too; as prosaic as the endless plain before us. It has no rise and fall; it goes at a walking pace. I understand Cavafy better now and I respect him for what he did.

...

The authorities arrive in the saloon. A dark-skinned lieutenant in a red fez holds in his hand a kind

1941

of whip with long horsehairs. I suppose it to be a mark of rank, but no: it is for flicking off flies, I am informed by my new friend, who grew up here. With the Arab is an Englishman in Egyptian uniform; he seems to be in charge. I ask him, when can we go ashore? Maybe tomorrow morning; the troops must be disembarked first.

"Can't we at least send word to the consul? We're carrying dispatches," I say to him.

"We'll see, we'll see . . ." is all his answer.

We wait for hours. The sun is going down. Suddenly here *is* the consul. He's the type that wants to be of service and show that he's in control. He goes to great lengths to make a fuss over us. He brings us ashore in the police launch, the lieutenant with the horse-tail whip travels with us. I ask him, for something to say:

"Do you have the black-out here?"

"My country is neutral," he replies to me in French, "but sometimes there are raids, so we observe the black-out."

How imperturbable they are, those neutrals!

We disembark at the hotel jetty. The rooms are large. From my window: the funnels and masts of large ships. A relaxing bath. Tomorrow morning we set out for Cairo. A good meal with the consul, who says to my wife, to cheer her up:

1941

"Why, you'll see your children* again in a week or so."

Our astonishment must have showed.

"Why, in a few more weeks the Germans will have taken everything. You'll be able to go back to Greece, then."

...

Saturday, 17 May. Cairo

We took the train at 8 in the morning for Cairo. The British won't let us go to Alexandria. For them, we are "evacuees." Our escort is a Canadian second-lieutenant who has probably never heard of Greece. In Cairo, at the railway station, even though the consul has telephoned ahead, no one turns up from the Greek Embassy or consulate, except for a couple of clerks. So we're handed over, with no possibility of escape, to the Canadian second-lieutenant and a British sergeant who between them seem determined to take us to the refugee camp. I show him our diplomatic passports, I try to make them understand that we've been charged by the Greek government with urgent telegrams that must be dispatched. Nothing. The only concession they will make to the three of us from the embassy is to take us in a taxi. As for the others, generals, elderly ladies, women with children, they load them all together, with a group of Maltese, into a lorry. It has the look of the tumbrel that bore Marie Antoinette to the guillotine. A sorry sight beneath the African sun.

...

Monday, 19 May. Cairo

Yesterday at the Pyramids. I felt nothing. Their abstract harmony is all on the outside. Inside, the hot, depressing climb up to the burial chamber.

Later, at the zoo: *Pelecanus onocrotalus*. Yellow, open beak. He stands by the hour without moving, clearly an intellectual.

...

Wednesday, 21 May. Hotel "Windsor," Alexandria

We left Cairo yesterday, at last. The sea, the joy of the sea.

...

Thursday, 22 May

Crete. They're going to take even Crete from us.

The English news: The Germans are dropping a whole army of parachutists. Fighting has broken out all

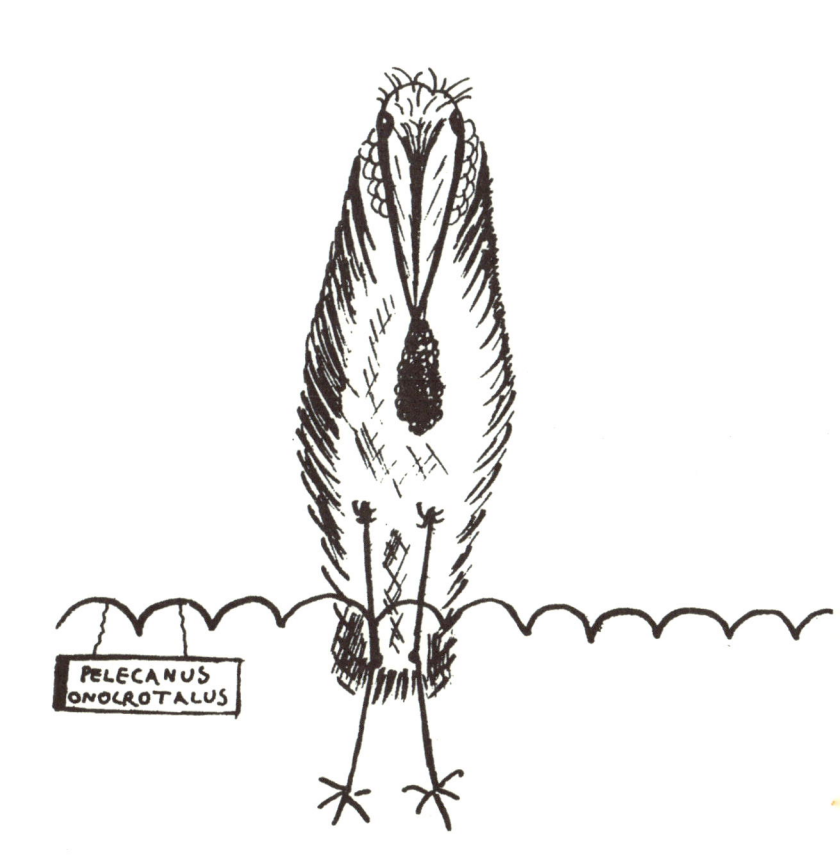

PELECANUS
ONOCROTALUS

over the island. For God's sake, when are the British going to be able to *do* something? They're so slow, so very slow. As often as not they behave as though they haven't woken up yet. Since Tuesday morning when the German attack began,* we've been losing ground all the time.

Tuesday, 27 May. Rue des Fatimites

... Disgusted up to here. If only I could have slept for 24 hours. I wish now I'd never left Greece, at times with terrible bitterness. That's where my friends are; those are my people over there.

...

Monday, 16 June. Cairo (Rue Monseigneur Coneboni)

We left the Rue des Fatimites by car at 7:30 with Mr. Georgiafentis and Mr. Tryphon Marangos. The one is director of a large commercial enterprise in Alexandria, the other his subordinate in Mehala Kebir. He spends ten months of each year in that little village. His spare time he devotes to Egyptology. He publishes his books on good-quality paper, in a few numbered copies. He was kind enough to take us all the way to Cairo, and then go back to his village, in this terrible heat.

1941

Truly, in Alexandria we found a few people who gave us their friendship, a friendship that for us made up for a great deal. Nanis first and foremost, and Timos,* and then some people who welcomed us as though they'd been expecting us for ages.

Last Sunday was taken up with farewells. On Saturday afternoon I went with Timos to see old Alexandria. We went by the Place des Consuls to the Rue de France and then to old parts of the city with leprous-looking housing, in streets so narrow the balconies were almost touching. Bleak, filthy places built round an area of cheap brothels. The area's been closed by the police; it was badly hit by bombs in the last raid. I'm told a dozen French sailors from the ships, neutral and mothballed in the harbor, were killed in those houses. I came face-to-face with despair on that walk; I kept remembering Blake's illustrations of Hell.

Sometimes you'd pass by little cafés, with three or four torpid Arabs smoking and the smell of hashish. Elsewhere you saw tiny shops with strange oriental merchandise. In one, hanging from the beam above the door, countless miniature bottles of every shape and color, covered in dust, as old as time, as moving as ancient libation-bowls. Another was a perfumery, the shop was called the Eye of Egypt. This eye, a terrible thing, was painted on it, and in the window a pile of powders for painting the human body. Particularly drawn by a stack of powders for the hair:

> *what distillation according to the recipes
> of ancient Helleno-Syrian magi . . .**

In that city you can't help thinking of Cavafy, gradually piecing together his impressions of all those little details, in every corner, and making out of them four or five poems a year. You have to go to Alexandria to understand the way Cavafy worked. Nowhere else could he have written: "we are a mixture of races here . . ." or "in part . . . in part"—not anywhere outside these streets with their dementing plethora of names you never heard before. It's a question, even, if he could have found, anywhere else, such a sense of stagnant dissolution, of the vanity of human efforts and the aestheticized nihilism that he knew so well how to convey in his poetry—that grace above all.

For myself, Alexandria reminded me of things from long ago in my childhood. Endless images of Smyrna emerged slowly before my eyes out of the depths of memory. At times like these, I felt rather like Phlebas the Phoenician, upon "entering the whirlpool."*

1941

Friday, 27 June. SS "Nieuw Amsterdam." Off Suez

... Cairo has gone. It gave me nothing.

Looking back now, nothing has stayed with me but the smell of camel-dung and a moldy taste. Perhaps also the long antennas of the boats on the Nile. That's all. I say nothing of the crowd of people I serve.*

What Egypt had to give me was Alexandria. It's a humbly commercial city. But there at least I felt, also, that I had fetched up in a corner of the greater Greek world. It was something to think, as I headed homewards, that I was treading the same street that began with the Gate of the Sun and ended at the Gate of the Moon and that somewhere along the Rue Nébi Daniel, a crazed mob had killed Hypatia.*

Yesterday I got to know Nikos Nikolaidis. I went to his studio with Elli Papadimitriou, who has a thing about the British and almost exploded when she heard the name of Palairet.*

"We're dispersing, we're dispersing," she said to me, once she knew we were leaving.* "And there are so few of us. But can't anything be done, in the name of God? I went and saw Tsouderos.* He's so wishy-washy, you don't like to push him too far; you end up feeling sorry for the man."

We took a taxi to find the Chareh el Wabour Faransaoui*—the street of the French steamship—in the

1941

Bulak quarter. The house is in an old narrow tenement-block; going up, it's like a minaret. Nikolaidis came to the door himself. He has the clean-shaven face of a Catholic priest and bushy white hair. His own paintings adorn the walls of the two tiny rooms. From the window, a sort of cross-roads and houses with balconies, with washing hung out to dry.

"It's like Italy, here," he said.

"Why should it be like Italy? Why shouldn't it be like Egypt?" demanded Elli.

"Italy, before the war, wasn't a bad place," he insisted.

He showed us his published books. His hands are soft, almost flaccid as he turns the pages. He showed us the edition he's preparing of a new work, by imprinting the manuscript onto waxed paper.* The initial capitals are ornamented, each one differently; the layout of each page will be different too.

"Do you send those to Greece?" I asked him.

"No. I allow nothing to distract me from the task at hand. Not even the pleasure of giving them to my friends. For me the work of art is like fucking. If it happens to result in children, that's purely by the way."

"But don't you think it's natural to care for our children?"

He looked at me.

"In order for me to take care of my work, I'd have to claim the place that belongs to me. And if I was to claim that place, it would mean having to play politics. And I don't want to play politics."

He got up from the "melancholy" divan with the old, crumpled cushions. He took down another volume, quarto in size, Ingres paper. He showed me the "justification": "This book is not for sale in Greece, as a protest at the imposition of censorship there." Elli was in a hurry and had to leave. We went down together and I kept company with him for another half hour, strolling in the midday streets. Two or three people I knew, whom we encountered, pretended not to recognize me. We talked about Cavafy.

"Give me your address," he asked me. "I'd like to send you some of my books."

I've never received the books. I've no idea what talent the man may possess. But the way he seemed to me, he left me with the impression of a "devotee of the spirit." In the midst of all the indescribable mess of our times, this man serves God and tries to keep alight a candle in the deserted chapel where chance has thrown him. The worth of his prayer is irrelevant. It's enough for me, for the moment, that it is a prayer.

1941

DAYS OF JUNE '41*

The new moon came out in Alexandria
with the old moon in her arms
as we were going towards the Gate of the Sun
in the darkness of the heart—three friends.
Who now would bathe in the waters of Proteus?
To change shape was something we wished for in youth
with longings that darted like great fish
in seas that turned suddenly foul;
we believed then in the body's omnipotence.
And now the new moon has come out holding
the old one in her arms; with the beautiful island
    bloodied
and wounded; the peaceful island, the mighty island,
    the innocent.
And the bodies like broken branches
and like roots torn up.

               Our thirst
a mounted sentry turned to marble
by the dark Gate of the Sun
does not know how to ask for anything: it keeps watch
an exile in these parts
close by the tomb of Alexander the Great.

Crete–Alexandria–South Africa, May–Sept. '41

1942

AN OLD MAN ON THE RIVER-BANK*

For Nanis Panagiotopoulos

And yet we need to consider in what manner we fare
    forward.
That you feel is not enough, neither that you think or
    move
nor that your body is in danger upon the ancient
    battlement,
while boiling oil and melted lead carve runnels in the
    stonework.

And yet we need to consider the direction in which we
    fare forward,
not as our pain would have it and our starving children
and the chasm of communication with our comrades
    on the farther shore;
and not the way it might be whispered by the blacked-
    out light in the makeshift hospital,
with the gleam of disinfectant on the pillow of the
    young man operated on at noon;
but in some other way, perhaps I mean just like

1942

the long river that comes out of the great lakes
    enclosed in the depths of Africa
and was once a god and then became a highway and
    benefactor and arbitrator and delta;
that is never again the same, as ancient wise men used
    to teach,
but maintains the same body always, the same course,
    the same compass-point,
its orientation the same.

I ask nothing else but to speak simply, to be granted
    this grace.
Because our song has become overloaded with so many
    kinds of music that slowly it is sinking
and our art has been overlaid so heavily that the gold
    has eaten away its face
and it is time we spoke the few words we have because
    tomorrow our souls set sail.

If to be human is to suffer, we are not human to suffer
    only
this is why I think so often, these days, of the great
    river
of this meaning that fares forward between banks of
    herbs and weeds

1942

and animals that graze and slake their thirst and people that sow and reap
and even of great tombs and small dwellings of the dead.
This flowing that follows its course and is not so different from human blood
or from human eyes when they gaze fixedly and without fear into their own hearts,
without the daily jitters over trivial things or even great ones;
when they gaze fixedly like the wanderer who has become used to measuring his progress by the stars,
not the way that we, looking into the closed garden of the drowsy Arab house the other day,
behind the lattice-screens, saw the cool courtyard change shape, grow larger and smaller;
changing as we watched, so did we change, the shape of our desires and of our hearts,
in the dewdrop of noon, ourselves the patient dough of a world that pursues us and molds us,
caught in the gilded nets of a life that was right and good but turned to ashes and sank into the sand
leaving behind it only that vague swaying, which made us queasy, of a lofty palm-tree.

Cairo, 20 June '42

1942

Cairo, at home: 7, Hishmat Pasha, Zamalek. Friday, 26 June

The next 48 hours will be crucial. The fate of Egypt hangs in the balance—and whether this war will go on for another five years or however many more. The British are holed up at Marsa Matruh; the Germans are looking for a place to strike. Panic has taken hold like a blaze in dry brushwood and is spreading. This so familiar form of panic, by now. I'm not like I was last year. I know now what people are like, how they behave in times like these. The only thing that depresses me: Whether the entire population of my country is wiped out, or only half of it, will now depend upon the idiocies of the British generals.

I have written nothing in this journal since I came to Cairo. All day long, pointless efforts as though you're swimming in sand, and then, in the evening, I'd come home filled with shame for the sorry state of the people who surround me: rogues and psychopaths or mental cripples. You have to make yourself into an Egyptian mummy if you're to put up with them. Meanwhile, events follow their fated course. They keep saying: "Hang on, we'll soon have everything fixed up nicely." I can hang on forever, if need be. But the war waits for no man.

1942

Tuesday, 30 June

Afternoon at the Anglo-Egyptian Club, to meet some British people on official business. Only Larry* was there, the others didn't turn up. A British officer, with very fair hair, was playing Beethoven sonatas on the veranda. A jackdaw was strutting over the lawn with its beak half-open like some dinner-suited idiot. The officer came over to us and cast a glance at the English newspaper Larry was reading. He made a few laughing comments about "stupid propaganda" and went out, carrying his sheaf of music.

"Thought I'd get in a bit of practice," he explained.

Such is the serenity of the Empire.

At the office: told I'm wanted by Kanellopoulos* on the telephone. I found a taxi and went. On the sofa in his office sat the heir to the throne.* Kanellopoulos tells me we're to leave Cairo tomorrow. So that's gone too, off we go once more, to beg our bread. Then to the British Embassy for details. For the moment we're being moved to Palestine.

Last Sunday at lunch, when it came up in conversation, Kanellopoulos said to me:

"There are two ways forward. One is to go to South Africa, that's the surer. Because if things go badly here, we'll have to be evacuated again from Palestine."

1942

I asked him which he was taking, himself?

He said he'd stick with the army.*

"Then I'm for Palestine too," I told him. "I may be able to make myself more useful than by going back to South Africa* on vacation."

He accepted that. But if we're going only such a short distance, why in such a hurry? Apparently the British are anxious to get us out. I'd heard this, when I told Kanellopoulos it can't be right to close down our consulates so soon, particularly the consulate in Alexandria.* But our own people want us out. My problem is I haven't the mentality of the hanger-on.

It's only a couple of days since a message came for me from Cook's: the things I'd sent by sea from South Africa were at Suez, what were they to do with them? I said, send them on to Cairo. A simple confession of faith. They'll be lost, now, along with so much else. I wonder about my books, in particular my Aeschylus, which for so many years has gone everywhere with me, and a Herodotus that I ordered from England, just before leaving Egypt for South Africa. We're perpetual refugees. OK, then. Let's be perpetual railway-porters too. OK again. But in the name of God, why must there be all this waste?

1942

Jerusalem, Hotel St. Louis. Sunday, 5 July

Continued from last Thursday. Anything, so as not to lose the habit of writing. I think I've written this before: these jottings aren't about the things that matter. More like the sorry traces we leave behind us, our cast-off clothes.

Thursday after lunch I telephoned Kanellopoulos, to say goodbye, we were leaving in the evening.

...

In the streets, the air of a city already abandoned to its new conqueror. At the British Embassy they were making bonfires of confidential documents in the garden; Arab taxi drivers were refusing to take British officers.

...

The "evacuation" train was due to leave at 21:00. We were there by 19:45. There was a set of empty third-class carriages and a motley throng of people waiting for the signal to start pushing and shoving through the turnstiles. The signal duly came, and all this wave of humanity, dragging along suitcases, paper bags, infants, sprang up and started pouring into the carriages, like water into a sinking ship. So we found ourselves on wooden seats in the midst of a crowd speaking German

1942

and Italian (the "free" subjects of the enemy), all getting on each other's nerves, quarrelling and shouting.

The train was blacked-out, it began to move. There were six of us in the compartment. The bitterness I felt was different from the pain I'd experienced when we left Crete. This was a humble, exhausted bitterness, it went right through me.

...

We reached Qantara, on the canal, after midnight, and stopped alongside a munitions train. On it were pasted notices: "No Lighting of Matches." We made our way slowly towards the sea, each one carrying what he could. While we were waiting for the ferry: bugles, rockets, red flares. An air-raid warning. The big iron raft came alongside, tied up, and we got on. To north and south we could see and hear the bombardment. Sometimes the drone of airplanes over our heads sent jitters through the crowd. Next to me a man started to shout in French:

"I say, you're standing between me and my wife! Do you mind, monsieur?"

It was some time before I realized it was me that he was addressing. I had no idea who he was or which one was his wife.

1942

The night was perfect, with a few small clouds in the east. So clear that when the morning star appeared, I took it at first for a flare. The alert was over. Beside us a bridge of boats connected the two banks. We decided we'd rather pass over into Asia on foot, and give the munitions train a wide berth. I untied my belt and strapped both our suitcases over my shoulders. I felt safer on the bridge. I reckoned that if anything happened, Maro and I could jump into the sea and haul ourselves out on one of the barges that made up the bridge. That way, too, we'd extricate ourselves from the human mass and put distance between ourselves and the munitions train, which was worrying me more than anything. As we came off the bridge and were going forward looking for the railway station, some British soldiers told us to turn to the left. We found ourselves entering a camp. An officer, elderly in appearance, pointed us towards a low white building:

"This way for caviar, truffles . . . and whatever else you do, scatter!" he said and burst out laughing, pleased with his little joke. "And watch out for scorpions."

We sat by a trench and waited. The signal was given at the end of the alert. It was beginning to get light (Friday, 3 July). There were soldiers sleeping on

1942

the sand. They got up slowly and went to wash at some standpipes set up in the open. It was very refreshing to watch their early morning high-spirits as they washed, half-naked. I went and shaved along with them. Later they gave us tea and sandwiches.

...

At 7:00 we learned that the train would start at 10:00. At 11:00 came the second invasion-wave, to capture seats, with frightful jostling and squabbling among the crowd that was by this time utterly exhausted. My Czech colleague gave up altogether and slit his wrists. All day without water and nowhere to stretch your legs. My right knee had gone to sleep. Maro was in a terrible state. And every so often I had to limp forward to the lead carriage, where Mr. Kollas was, and the compartment of the British brigadier in charge of the escort, just to make sure we didn't end up shunted into some refugee camp. I'd learned something about that from last year's experience.

We had no idea, even, where they were going to offload us; that was a military secret. At last, well into the night, we learned that the terminus was to be Jerusalem. I was suffering badly from hunger. I found the discomfort to be less if I stood upright in a corner. For the first time in my life, I fell asleep in that position.

It was a half-waking state of suspension, which was broken when the train stopped at a station. Looking round me then, I saw an elderly woman, huddled to one side, talking to a friend from Alexandria. She was crying loudly. I went up to her.

"I'm quite strong," she said, "but my body can't take any more. I feel I just can't keep going any longer . . ."

She spoke in excellent French. I sat down opposite her and made conversation.

"Are you French?" I asked her.

"No," she said, "*je suis italienne antifasciste.* My husband was a Fascist. He knew the leaders of the Fascist movement personally. But I could never understand why they did the awful things they did. I left when my brother decided to leave Alexandria. He was in the antifascist movement. And I've left my daughter behind, she's separated, she's got young children. Oh, what an awful thing . . ."

Her voice was barely audible. I could think of nothing else to say, so in a few words I told her my own story. I may have helped her calm down somewhat. I remember that conversation well, between two fleeing strangers on that blacked-out train as it crept slowly forward into the empty night of Palestine.

1942

We arrived here at 04:00 (Saturday, 4 July). We were lucky to avoid the camp. The consul was waiting for us at the station. He took us to the great Jerusalem hotel, the King David. The large hall with Cretan motifs on the ceiling was a generic backdrop for any kind of tragedy you liked.

...

There were three beds left in the dining room. I gave them up to an embassy employee, who was ill, his wife, and a girl from the office. Maro and I, many telephone calls later, found ourselves billeted eventually in a small hotel belonging to German Jewish refugees, where I write now. Jerusalem at night was a blacked-out and unspeaking city full of cars, the sort that made you think of Al Capone, there was something brutal and sleazy about them. I slept gratefully until late in the afternoon.

Monday, 6 July

Until the evening of the day before yesterday, Jerusalem was for me a closed box, and I'd no desire to see inside it. Around me were voices speaking German or other tongues with a German accent; that was all. Then yesterday morning we went walking in the Old City. In the narrow streets of the bazaar I found images like fairy-tales that enticed me from beyond my childhood, beyond birth. Looking into the patina of the faces in this crowded hive, I felt suddenly what a scandalous thing in life is a European. The idea of a Messerschmitt in this environment is a monstrous thing. We say we're fighting for European civilization. European civilization is bankrupt now, once and for all, thanks to this present war. European civilization means Germany, whose acts are perfectly European, that is to say scientific. They kill us, they dismember us, they lay waste our country in accordance with all the laws of science. And let's not quibble: the others, the flabby ones who say, "let's see" or "maybe we ought to throw in the towel," stand for nothing at all. They've turned out to be not so much the defenders of Europe, as the last dregs of something that's already over and done with. There's nothing to be saved out of this civilization, so let it go: what we have to save is mankind, if we can.

These were my thoughts as I went through the confused alleys of the bazaar yesterday, and I felt my fate placed, as that of the Greeks has always been, at the exact point where the balance tips between Greece and the East; as if I'd been sent to sit in judgment on what should be allowed to pass out of here, and through the portals of Europe, from this dark and enchanted world.

1942

In Egypt, the war seems to be going better. Hopes of returning to Cairo.

Thursday, 16 July

There are various groups of Greeks here who heartily detest one another. All of them work for British agencies that have some hand in Greek affairs, or are used by them in some way.

...

Sometimes I have the impression, the alarming impression, that all of us who are away from Greece are an insubstantial troupe of madmen. And the drama, the great drama, is that the people who go mad, and as time goes on lose their substance, are the best of them. Because the others are felons with malice aforethought.

Their passion for not letting go, not to be left behind by their country, becomes a political rant that's exploited by the cold-hearted and clever ones. And none of them can see, in the midst of this unspeakable crucible in which we're all seething, the difference, the unbridgeable difference: that those back there in Greece are suffering in their bodies every day, every night, while the ones here talk and shout.

1942

This sick bunch of Greeks that have congregated here outside occupied Greece. Not only those who fled at the beginning but also those who keep on coming. Were they perhaps different back there? You see them in your mind's eye: starting out in their little boats from Attica, the Aegean islands, then arriving in Turkey and making their way to Egypt. As they go, something about them alters, they begin to resemble us, you can see the transformation happening. What is going on? What can it be that made them so different, back there? What makes them change when they get here? Could it be our nostalgia—our malaise?

I'm giving too much importance, I suppose, to emotional motives. But isn't it emotional motives, to a large extent, that make wars happen, and still more situations like this modern Greek diaspora? Without these motives, how could we have held on as long as we did in Albania?* Now the mechanism has gone into reverse, the spirits of these people are being worked up like a bull in the last stages of the bull-fight.

...

1942

Saturday, 18 July

Yesterday with the Edwardses. We started out at the King David Hotel.

...

Lunch at the Vienna. Edwards was telling us the story of the ship, the *Struma*. A rotten hulk, flying the Panamanian flag, sets out from some harbor in Romania. A small ship, loaded so heavily that its passengers, about a thousand fleeing Jews, have no room to sit down, and take turns going up for a breather on the narrow deck. In this way they come to Haifa. The authorities in Palestine, for fear of the Arabs, won't accept them. Jewish organizations come forward and offer to house all these people in a camp, for the duration of the war; they even offer to meet the cost. Nothing doing. The ship is turned back. It arrives at Istanbul. The Turks won't let anyone off, not even for a few hours. No gangplank is allowed, either. The people on board survive on food provided in baskets let down on ropes from the quayside. With delays and excuses six months go by. In the end the Turkish authorities decree the ship must leave. So those ravaged bodies set out back into the Black Sea. They're far from land when a storm strikes, the ship splits and sinks. There were only forty survivors, according to the story.

1942

What sort of a civilization is this of ours, that allows things like that to happen?

...

Sunday, 19 July

... Today at the Holy Sepulchre, to look at it a little on my own, after the first visit with the deacon Stephanos, a few days ago. At times I feel shame at my ignorance and lack of emotional preparation in the midst of this biblical landscape.

I try to articulate the unimaginable complexity of this church. I try to effect the subtraction required so as to understand that while I'm standing under the dome of a church, I have to imagine at the same time that no roof exists and that here is the place of the Deposition, here the Tomb, and over there, where I'll go in a little while, by some stone steps, is Golgotha.

This is an archaeology the exact opposite of what we're used to in Greece. There, the archaeologists have so scientifically cleared everything away from the dwellings of the dead gods: here you see the equivalent of an Acropolis of Athens, but where nothing has been displaced of all that had accrued over the years, where even the harems of the Turks have been left alone and the churches of the Christians untouched, and then the

1942

whole thing enclosed in a building complex from the beginning of the last century.

At Golgotha two sailors in the uniform of the Greek navy. They're being shown round by a monk and listening to him with the kind of rapture you see on children's faces when the fairy-tale begins. He takes a flower from the altar and gives it to them.

"Can't you spare me a bit of candle from the Holy Sepulchre as well?" one of them asks.

...

Around the Holy Sepulchre, where they sell souvenirs to the pilgrims, I saw a shop, its name must have been Italian, and in one corner a gigantic pile: "crowns of thorns" for sale.

In the afternoon we went down, following the walls of the Old City, and sat above a gully opposite the Mount of Olives. Beautiful colors.

As we went past, in a corner, behind some railings, we saw a heap of watermelons like the heads of executed prisoners, green above the honey-color of the old stone.

All the time my mind is turning over the strange phenomenon that is this war, so lacking in spirit, so glum, without even a song of its own (I speak of the West). And all the time there are these breeding-grounds for failure and despondency in human beings, in events. Why?

...

Wednesday, 22 July

Afternoon with Elli Papadimitriou.*

...

On the way back we saw a group of Greek sailors. With them were two Orthodox priests. One of the priests ran towards us, in a terrible state, and told us that a few streets back an Australian truck had overturned, injuring twelve, two of them seriously. They'd been taken to hospital, where one of them was to have his leg amputated, the doctors had decided. Their comrades were muttering around us, looking daggers.

We went on our way, talking of the wretched condition of so many people in need of some kind of care, here so far from home: the wounded, the sick, the discharged soldiers with nowhere to lay their heads. The whole country is starving, help doesn't come easily. But what about this? People who should be useful are turned loose, to mutter their resentment through the streets, while it's the idiots that keep their posts. Where has the engine broken down? We're at the end of our tether.

1942

Elli has a story:

Four soldiers with psychiatric disorders are taken to a British hospital. Soon one of them is well enough to be let out into the garden. As luck would have it, there's a chameleon out there. And the chameleon gives our friend the idea of putting a cigarette into its mouth, to see how it smokes. The reptile snuffs it. An English nurse has been watching from an upstairs window. Quick as a flash, she's summoned four hefty warders, who proceed to beat the unfortunate experimenter black-and-blue. "Not because they were angry," Elli explained, "but to punish him, for cruelty to animals."

Now try and make that sick man and his friends understand the British mentality. Elli goes on:

In another hospital there's one of ours, a Greek soldier. He's a tall lad with a neat black mustache. When the time comes and he's sent for convalescence—it's the system there—he's given a job to do. His is to collect the garbage. Nobody's being mean to him. It would have been the same if he'd been British. But this kid doesn't know any English, and there's no one to explain it to him. So he gets the idea it's meant as an insult. He goes about his task in the most terrific huff, all the time muttering: "Every bit of garbage passes through *Greek* hands . . . Every bit of garbage passes through *Greek* hands . . ."

The British have their character and the Greeks have theirs too, for good and ill both. If it hadn't been for that, we'd never have come through the snows of the campaign in Albania with a crumb of dry biscuit and half a blanket. But this resentment that simmers everywhere—there are plenty who exacerbate it, but no one thinks to soothe it.

Jews. It's as though they've suffered so much, nothing touches them any more. One tells you his thoughts on the problem of Europe. He finds that certain states stand in the way of the general plan: "Kill the lot of them," he says, deadpan. Another: You're telling him about Greece. You tell him about the famine there. You tell him that people are forced to eat donkeys and dogs. This makes no impression. "So long as they've still got donkeys and dogs," he concludes, in the mildest manner.

Friday, 24 July

The word is, we'll be going back to Cairo soon. The signs are good. This waiting is paralyzing.

I've started writing something* since yesterday; but it's blocked.

...

1942

It's been a fortnight. It seems like yesterday: Friday (the 10th), we made our excursion to the River Jordan and the Dead Sea.

The mountains of Moab; no lift to the spirits.

First stop, at the foot of the Mountain of the Forty Days, outside Jericho. The little farm belongs to the monastery: a small orchard. Trees and a fast-flowing stream. The high, sheer cliff above, the place of the Temptation on the Mountain; the monastery is squeezed halfway up the cliff-face. We took the path. The monastery is half constructed, half excavated out of the rock, like a hollow tooth. We asked the abbot how many years had he been there. "No more than fifty," he replied. A delightful old man. The monks have a hard life. They told us about the last Arab uprising, when the monastery was sacked and the monks ill-treated. They showed us a cave, a great secret cellar to keep their grain safe. A wooden flour-mill was placed so as to conceal the entrance. They told us that during the last war there had been battles fought down there on the plain, below the monastery, you couldn't be too careful. The steward is from Crete. A shy man, though past sixty. He laughs and blushes. He asked us where had we come from. When we told him, from Cairo, he said:

"Scared, then, were you?" and burst out laughing.

1942

He's very proud of his pocket-watch, he keeps fingering it lovingly, in the fold of his cassock.

Down at Jericho, another monastery. In the garden, the sycamore of Zacchaeus, so they tell you. Jericho is a small low-lying place with fruit trees. Its walls have disappeared, ever since the famous trumpet-blast.

We headed towards the mountains, towards the Jordan. Hot and stifling, everywhere here: everything empty, somehow non-human, down here below sea-level.

The monastery of St. John the Baptist was damaged in an earthquake a few years back. All the upper story is in ruins. Two monks, all in all.

Abbot Onouphrios, from Sparta, is fair-haired. He put on his stole and led us into the baptistry. The yellow waters of the River Jordan roll by, a little way below. You don't see them at first, until you're almost on top of them. At the river's edge, tied up to the branch of a tree, a little sea-going sailboat, its red paint faded. When Greece was overrun by the Germans, three monks set sail from the Holy Mountain, Mount Athos,* in this little craft. They'd sailed for ninety days until they reached the shores of Palestine. I wonder how many days it must have taken them to get through the formalities and be allowed to land. Then, with those travails behind them,

1942

they'd loaded their little ship onto a lorry and brought it here, to the river where Christ was baptized. We got in, all together, with the abbot and some sailors from the Greek navy, for the sacrament of baptism.*

Afterwards we ate at the monastery. The second monk had prepared the meal. He was tall and slim as a sapling. He was from Megara.*

"I'll excommunicate him!" the abbot threatened, when the food was late in arriving.

He answered back: "I fought in the Balkan Wars, in 1912. Nobody excommunicates me."

In the chapel on Golgotha, the other day, another monk, huddled in a dark corner, like a ghost, said to me, "Twenty years I've guarded this slab, to preserve it from the feet of the Franks."*

The bare feet of the Megarian who was looking after us were bloodied. These people are poor. I wondered how people die, in these places.

The Dead Sea is another story. The mountains that enclose it in the distance are pale blue. As you approach, looking across at them, it's like entering a spa town. We stopped at the hotel, a modern contrivance. We were very thirsty. Further down was a harbor for sea-planes. The first thing you notice about the Dead Sea is the silence. Its water is almost the color of lead, it repels the human in you. Still, I decided to try it. I undressed in a bathing-cabin. On my way down, I could feel the dry salt on the boardwalk, thick and sharp. When you try swimming, you feel as though you're not in water but in a different element that obstructs you and pushes your body upwards towards the surface. Only your head is at liberty to sink. But then, when you let it, your eyes, nostrils, and palate are seared by the salt, your hair feels as though it's clogged with glue. It has a bitter taste, this liquid. But what makes the greatest impression of all, an impression almost of horror, is the total absence of any living thing around you. Not only are there no fish or water-insects, but no seaweed either, not the slightest fuzz of green on the pebbles on the bottom. You feel yourself to be a grotesque exception, a living being, in the midst of this liquid death.

At the Monastery of the Forty Days, they showed us the rock where Christ had been sitting, when he was visited by Satan. A tiny church was built over the rock, and on the wall, to the left, was hung a notice with the relevant passage from the Gospel, in English, and beneath it, in block capitals, also in English:

THIS IS THE PLACE GENTLEMEN

This "gentlemen," that you've got used to seeing on notices in other places in England, and to hearing in other circumstances, came as a slap in the face. A symbol, too, of the impenetrable mess we're living through now: a prank of the crudest kind.

Monday, 27 July

Yesterday morning at the Wailing Wall. Maro and I threaded the alleyways of the Old City, as twisted as an intestine, as somebody once said. We were almost lost when a little boy with a tray on his head, in return for baksheesh, showed us the way. We'd taken several turnings and were beginning to think we'd been made fools of, when we heard a distant sound like water running in a deep cistern. We turned one more time and found ourselves in front of the wall, which stood bare in the light of the sun. At the foot of the wall were not many people. A young woman, sitting, was crying quietly. An old man with a look of Gémier in the role of Shylock wailed more loudly, at the same time beating his breast with his hands and sometimes his head against the stones of the wall. Further along, two or three young men, standing, the ultra-traditional sort with long sidelocks, were howling, holding some sort of prayerbook in their hands, making rhythmical movements like someone soothing an infant. A memorable "catharsis."

...

1942

STRATIS THALASSINOS* AT THE DEAD SEA

> *Sometimes you see in remote chapels, built in legendary landscapes, the relevant passage from the Bible, written in English, and beneath it:*
> "THIS IS THE PLACE GENTLEMEN!"*

Jerusalem, unruled city, city adrift,
Jerusalem, city of refugees.

Sometimes at midday
on the asphalt road you see sweep by
a flock of black leaves scattered—
Migrating birds go past beneath the sun
but you do not raise your head.
Jerusalem, unruled city, city adrift!

Babel tongues, unknown,
without affinity to grammar
to saint's life or psalter
whose syllables you learned one autumn
while by the mole the fishing boats made fast;
unknown tongues that stuck
like cigarette butts dead on ravaged lips.

Jerusalem, city of refugees!

1942

But their eyes speak all the same language,
not the Word that became man, dear God look kindly
    on us,
not journeys to see new places, but
the dark train full of fugitives, where infants
are fed on filth, and the sins of their parents
and the middle-aged can sense the chasm
opening out between the body
that remains behind like a wounded camel
and the soul whose courage knows no bounds, or so
    they say.
It is also the ships that take them on voyages,
standing-room only like stuffed prelates
packed into the hold, to come to rest one evening
in the seaweed of the deep, so very gently.

> Jerusalem, unruled city, city adrift!
> Into the River Jordan
> three monks one day came sailing,
> and on the bank made fast
> a red, three-masted sailboat.
> Three months these three did sail
> from Athos, Holy Mountain,
> and made fast to a branch
> upon the Jordan's bank:

1942

      the penance of the refugee.
      For three months going hungry
      for three months going thirsty,
      for three months keeping vigil
      and from the Holy Mountain came,
      and from Salonica they came,
      from slavery, those monks.

All of us are like the Dead Sea
so many fathoms below the level of the Aegean.
Come with me, and I will show you the place:

      In the Dead Sea
      there are no fish
      there is no seaweed
      not even a sea-urchin's spine,
      for nothing lives in brine.

      These are not living things
      that have a stomach
      to feel hunger
      that grow nerves
      to suffer pain or anger,

THIS IS THE PLACE, GENTLEMEN!

1942

> In the Dead Sea
> contempt
> is every man's
> commodity,
> what an oddity!
>
> Heart and mind
> grow stiff with salt
> so bitter,
> until like minerals
> they glitter,

THIS IS THE PLACE, GENTLEMEN!

> In the Dead Sea
> your friends and foes
> your child, your wife
> and all those dearest
> you'll find at rest.
>
> Gone to Gomorrah
> down on the seabed
> and the nearest
> thing to happy, not expecting
> any letters here.

1942

GENTLEMEN,
let us proceed upon our tour
so many fathoms beneath the level of the Aegean.

July '42

Ο ̔ Στράτης Θαλασσινός
εἰς τή Νεκρή Θάλασσα.

«Κάποτε βλέπεις σε πυρεκκλη-
σία, χτισμένα πάνω στις θρυλικές
τοποθεσίες, τή σχετική περιγραφή
τξ Εὐαγγελίε γραμμένη ἀγγλικά
καί ἀποκάτω: THIS IS THE PLACE
GENTLEMEN.'))._ Ἰόλιος '42.
(γράμμα τξ Σ. Θ. ἀπο τήν Ἱερυσαλήμ)

ΑΙΓΑΙΟΝ ΠΕΛΑΓΟΣ

Ἱερυσαλήμ, ἀκυβέρνητη πολιτεία,
Ἱερυσαλήμ, πολιτεία τῆς προσφυγιᾶς.

1942

Sunday, 2 August

Tuesday we leave, if no other obstacles present themselves. This morning at the Holy Sepulchre to pay our respects. Negro soldiers. A white man is explaining, the black sergeant translates. Their eyes widen, looking at the slab of the Deposition; awe on their faces. Perhaps they're the only ones who are like the little children, as the Gospel has it.

The Church of the Twelve Apostles. An old Russian woman opens the doors for us. She's been away from Russia twelve years. Beautiful icon-screen of carved wood, painted. White curtains, spotlessly clean. I asked her who looks after them like that.

"I do, who else? I wash and iron them," she says in her accented Greek.

At the monastery of the Twelve Apostles—remember—looking down from above: at the back the Last Supper, a large painting done without artistry, covering the entire wall, and at right angles to the painting, a long marble table, the spitting image of the painted one. Hardly any light, even though it was midday. A bald monk, with lethargic movements, was setting out knives and forks and cutting slices from a watermelon. How the red color stood out. On the edge of the table below the icon, two large watermelons, brilliant green.

At the city walls, and then the Museum of Folk Art. Whatever the hands of man take up with love is holy.

Cairo. Wednesday, 5 August

... We arrived at 01:00, today. As far as Lydda by car, then the train from there. For hours on end I watched the desert sand. It gives you a feeling rather like the sea, that bare, sterile, uninhabitable outlook. Its stark ridges, camel trails, and whenever there's a breath of wind small tornadoes whip madly across it like whirlpools. After the canal, it was dark on the train, the journey tedious. It all seems like child's play after our exodus a month ago. In Cairo—with Haroula who had travelled with us—we got badly lost in the darkened streets. The Arab taxi driver couldn't find the hotel. In the end we found it, but our telegram had never arrived. Phone calls. Everywhere was full. After an hour we were offered a pension that had two rooms vacant. "Pension Adolf," they told us it was called. Actually, it was the Adelphi, but it did rather have the air of an Adolf or a Gustav. Something between a cabaret and a brothel that might have been decorated by de Chirico or Salvador Dalí when drunk. In the hall was a small bar with a plywood cut-out of a painted woman. At the bar some sort of pimp with a Free French second-lieutenant and another specimen.

The strangest thing was the corridor that led to our rooms. Rather like toy cubes that fit inside one another. The first cube was full of empty drawers and in the corner a tailor's dummy stark naked. Then a bathroom with a bidet. There was a toilet, basins, tiles, everything polished and gleaming. But all over these necessary objects were small handwritten notices: "Clients are requested not to use." Then came our rooms, where we got to sleep as best we could at about 03:00. We left first thing in the morning.

Wednesday, 12 August

In the morning, to the Ministry of War.* Kanellopoulos is supposed to be going towards Alexandria to meet up with a section of the First Brigade on its way to its new position on the Desert Front.

We were held up at the Ministry by the usual hangers-on: royalty, generals, people with papers to be signed. We got on the road to Alexandria about 12:30. That heavy Egyptian sun. Pointed sails: the Nile with its primordial craft. Water-buffaloes, or *gamouzes*, as the Greeks of Egypt call them. Camels carrying entire households swaying on their backs: great copper trays, a trunk filled with gaily painted pots, a mattress, and perched on top of everything, the owner's wife. Women with purple marks on their chins, riding on donkeys. Fields green with growing corn. Sometimes tall palm-trees, seeming to walk on air. Mud huts. Naked Arab children plunging into the water—the noontime, the light, and the August heat here by the great river and the desert.

We went in two cars. On the way, we asked the British military police, in their red peaked-caps, if they'd seen the Greeks—"The Greek Convoy" (a section of the Greek Brigade on its way to the front). After an hour and a half of this, outside a village, the first dusty vehicle with the blue insignia cut with a mauve horizontal band and the head of the goddess Athena: they were ours. We went on, asking for the officer in charge. We pass cars, tractors towing artillery, more cars. These Greek faces look different from the ones you'd have seen on parade in the streets of Athens, before the war. Being so far from home gives them a different air. They look like students, or volunteers of 1821.* Some are stripped to the waist, stretched out asleep in that blinding glare. They've been on the road for six or seven days now, all the way from the desert of Palmyra; today since 05:00. It's siesta time. The metal of the vehicles is as hot as a pan on the stove. A lot of the men are shut up inside. The ones looking out at us have serious, cheerful faces.

1942

"Splendid material we've got here," the colonel says, when at last we find him, "and damned hard to keep in order: every man of them *thinks*, they wonder about things."

I'm thinking of the sound of Greek arms that will be heard once more, soon, after sixteen months. Of Greek warriors once again on this soil, in the footsteps of Synesios of Ptolemaïs, in the footsteps of Heraclius.*
I'm remembering, too, the lines:

> *Not by stones nor wood nor craft*
> *of builders is the city made, but by*
> *its men wheresoe'er they be.* *

For us, now, *they* are our *city*.

Wednesday, 26 August. 07:30

It must be years since last I tried to write at such an hour. From the open window, behind me, comes a cataract of sounds that I've never, since we came to this hotel, been able to get used to. The Arabs, the trams, the traffic, everything leaks noise. We both sleep badly. I think with bitter nostalgia of our house in Zamalek, which we lost in our mad exodus to Palestine. Panel-

1942

beaters, klaxons, engines, newspaper-sellers—it's like the end of the world out there. I'm reminded again of the image of the ant struggling uphill with an enormous weight. It runs away from him, and he starts over, again and again. The same image as I had a year ago.

What business has a "sensitive" (in the technical sense) person in the midst of all this?

Work has been heavy, since we came, with many difficulties, and non-existent resources. Much of the time is wasted. You lie down at night and look back at your day, drained dry like a glass of water. You don't know what's happened, what use any of it has been.

Even in this diary I haven't been able to write more often.

Last Saturday, the 22nd, telephone call from the British Embassy:

"This afternoon at 6. To meet a distinguished person."*

Doors and portals with sentries and servitors, until you reach the inner garden. An English lawn bright green and at the end of it a triangular sail, poking up from the invisible river beyond. Various people from the newspaper world were gathered. Suddenly all conversation ceased. The signal had been given to go in. In the ballroom, a great chamber apparently in the process of being painted, in front of an exceedingly small table, hunched up like Rodin's *Thinker*, except for his head that was watching and following everything, sat Churchill. He wore mauve dungarees; held in his hand, like a stubby pencil, was a long cigar. With all this crowd around him, he looked somehow smaller, as though at the far end of an enormous lecture-theater. Then he spoke and came closer. At the end, when it was time for questions, some reporter wearing a fez asked him what he thought of Rommel.

"That is the way of generals," he replied, "sometimes to advance, sometimes to retreat. Why, no one knows . . ."

Saturday, 5 September

Yesterday we returned from Alexandria, where we'd been since last Saturday.

I'd gone with Kanellopoulos to visit the Greek Brigade, now encamped in its new positions. The morale of the boys is impressive, the ease with which those mountaineers and islanders adapt themselves to every new circumstance, whether of climate or the machinery of war. You see them working in the desert

1942

sand, in the terrible heat, laying mines, testing their wireless, as easily as they would in their own villages.

Timos* was vehement, stubborn, well-meaning, as always. He insists on making out that Cavafy's "Theodotos" is an obscure poem. I try to explain to him how I understand it; he won't be persuaded—

> *And do not delude yourself that in your life*
> *so circumscribed, well-ordered, and plain boring,*
> *spectacular or dreadful things don't happen.*
> *Perhaps this very moment at the door*
> *of some neighbor's well-kept apartment knocks—*
> *unseen, ethereal—Theodotos,*
> *and enters with just such a severed head.**

The final proposition has nothing to do with the beginning of the poem, insists Timos. Impossible to convince him that the poet is telling us transparently that evil affects not only important people, but insignificant householders too, indeed anyone. At that moment the waiter put down a tray on the table with four beefsteaks.

"Are they good?" I ask him.

"Dripping blood, sir, a perfect treat. Such a treat, so bloody!"

1942

"And that," I tell Timos, "is precisely what Cavafy meant."

But he thinks I'm laughing at him.

Timos, who has a mania for tracking down Cavafy's sources, in the manner of someone doing battle with time or with some unseen enemy as he walks down the street, tells me that Cavafy once said what a good idea it would be to put together an anthology of forgotten verses, and gave as an example these ones:

> *The flower-beds of yesteryear*
> *are fallen into the sere,*
> *and laughter is extinguished quite,*
> *the young with age grown white.*

Lines written by my father.* He adds that Mrs. Zelita had heard Cavafy say:

"They're lines by some poet from Smyrna—the best forgotten verses I know."

Wednesday, 16 September. 05:30

Awake since 04:00; I can't sleep. I heard the sounds of the street start up, one by one: horseshoes on the asphalt, the first trams—a terrific clatter of ironmongery—cars. This hotel is the noisiest place I've ever known in my life.

1942

Opening my eyes in bed—there's no let-up in the torment from the trivial humiliations of my daily life. Frayed nerves—perhaps. But this ability of our surroundings to plunge us up to the neck in mud, to wear us out with meaningless trivia. Maybe it was always like this, but in today's world it's a scandal. The life ✓ we're living gives me the impression sometimes of a lit candle, left behind in an empty room. Melting down to no purpose.

Since April of last year, when we left Greece, this is my first autumn.* All the months that have gone by: a heavy summer, a strange one, outside the rhythm of the seasons.

Friday, 18 September

To Mr. and Mrs. Lachovaris' place. They always have company with them. A spindly Englishwoman, saying nothing, knitting. She's going to teach Maro the language. An Englishman with fair hair and the look of an intellectual—he looks younger than he is in reality—is fairly quiet too, then bursts into speech. We discuss the life of the Arabs, old houses in Cairo, the tales of the *Thousand and One Nights*. He says the Egyptians don't like it if you talk to them about this book. They think it "indecent": they're almost ashamed of it. But when it comes down to it, they're ashamed of everything.

Outside, it sounds like the end of the world, with shouting and soldiers singing. By now the nights are very cool, almost cold. Exhaustion every evening. Not real tiredness, more from nerves. Impression of swimming through mud. Perhaps, of course, all this may pass. Above all, there's a lack of people. And among the few who remain, most are mad.

Sunday, 20 September

There's a lack of *useful* people. Noxious ones there are in plenty: middle-men, diggers, egotists, tight-rope walkers, idle prattlers, mental cripples, leave-me-alone types, parasites, and so many more. Once upon a time they didn't count for anything, or if they did, nobody cared. Now they've become a plague. Because the rest are humiliated, mutilated, and everything enflames their wounds.

We had lunch with the Lachovaris couple. They have a *house*. It's like all houses that have had a natural existence and seem such extraordinary things to those of us who live constantly on the move: things that have belonged to people who have lived and passed on, old photographs, books that have remained for years in the same place. The wife has infinite sensitivity; she comes from the Greek islands. The husband—it seems scandalous that anyone can be so honest in these times of ours—has an inexhaustible love, which he insists on dressing up in the garb of scientific logic. His reason tells him there's no future for the absurd. Does he or doesn't he know what he is himself?

We stayed with them until late. After tea they asked us if we'd like to listen to music. I looked at the catalogue of their record collection, a meticulously kept little notebook. The choice was good. I listened to the introduction to Bach's Second Suite, which for so many years has always kept the same freshness for me; the second movement of the Seventh;* Capriccio by Stravinsky. Listening to music nowadays makes me miserable; instead of relaxing me, it affects me badly.

"Paris has become a German brothel under pain of death," I read in today's Greek newspaper.

...

Wednesday, 30 September

This time last year we hadn't yet moved into our house in Pretoria. It would take another month of smudging papers with ink until I could regain the habit of writing. That lasted until January. Then we were on the move again. The little writing-desk, which made it this far, is shut up now in a room in Sharia Emad-el-

1942

Din,* like a broken piano. Dear God, look kindly on our weaknesses. Here in the Middle East, as it's called, we're sinking all the time. We're not people any more, we're *exiles*. But we don't all share the same exile; there are as many conditions of exile as there are of us. We're the crew of a ship that's gone down, each one fighting for his life, each one separately, astride his own piece of flotsam.

...

1942

Last Saturday night I stayed late at the office, working. A night of tragedy. Not the air raid, though it was spectacular enough; not the shop on the corner opposite, that went up in flames; but this:

In the early hours of the morning I heard a loud bang from the street. I went out onto the balcony and saw that two cars had collided at the cross-roads in front of the building. Both had stopped, no sign of life. A few moments later, just like a match flaring, one of the cars caught fire. An Arab jumped out, flames streaming from his *gellabia*. He leapt in the air, stopped, rolled over and over on the pavement, then took to his heels once more. Other Arabs were hitting at the car with sticks. By this time it had become an inferno. Perhaps they were trying to help the people trapped inside. It must have been a good ten minutes before the fire brigade arrived. I still had before my eyes the image of a charred mouse I'd once seen, when I read in the morning newspapers that the driver and his passenger had been burnt to ashes.

1942

Sunday, 11 October

Heat and dreadful humidity. Ten o'clock at night, after dinner. Nerves snapping from the racket outside. Trams, bells, squeals of brakes, cornets, gramophones, Arab voices, horses' hooves, clanging metal—you'd think it had all been planned, just to spite you, specially.

Yesterday at Buckley's,* for cocktails. Three small rooms filled with human bodies, all of them bathed with sweat. You feel like a piece of cabbage boiling in the pan. I've rarely been in such poor spirits.

Today is Bairam.* We went to sign official books at various palaces. Fezes and redingotes, caftans. Atmosphere of a great oriental festival, managed somehow, *neutrally*, in the midst of our war-fever.

...

This afternoon I stayed in the hotel, doing nothing at all but muttering and drawing pencil lines on paper. This made me feel better. I needed it.

Saturday, 24 October

All day in bed. Since the day before yesterday I've had a fever. It's the first time, since our return to Cairo, that I've spent so many hours away from the office.

Today's bulletin: "Attack by the Eighth Army last night with air support. Fierce fighting continues."*

This is the battle that we've been waiting for, for so long. We need significant successes here in Africa, before operations in Russia become frozen by winter. What successes?

Afternoon at 17:00, to Public Relations, Col. Philpots. In his office a file is waiting. He reads from it: "Greeks fighting well. Fifty prisoners taken." The news will be released in 2-3 days. He can't be persuaded to release it sooner.

...

Tuesday, 27 October

At home. This biological feeling of disgust that rises sometimes and suffocates me. In the restaurant downstairs, I was observing the dreadful ugliness that surrounds us. Images passed chaotically before my eyes: great halls of theaters, full of people, in darkness before a brilliantly lit stage, where some performance was going on, music was playing. Books; pages of books held insistently open at such-and-such a place—I was that man, who was so moved by these things that he was discussing among his friends. What are we coming to, in this whirlwind? What have we become? I feel like shouting. And now as I write, I hear only one answer, the lamentation of Aeschylus' chorus:

Cry sorrow sorrow . . .

Their criticism—of others—is made not in order to arrive at any object, but so that when the time comes they can say they have made it. For them what matters is not how they ought to act at this moment, but to be able to say, when they go back to Greece, "We told you so." And they talk, and talk, and never stop. But when you ask them, "Today, here in exile, while the war is going on, what do you want to happen?" they answer with grimaces that mean nothing. They are like people who want to salvage some capital, great or small, for after the war, but fail to understand that everything we own and everything that exists, even we ourselves, through the merest accident, either now or in a little while, may be lost forever.

Wednesday, 18 November

I must make up my mind to this, once and for all: seriousness and politics are two perfectly separate things.

Sunday, 22 November

Evening before last, on my way in to Shepheard's, I met Leland Stowe.* He'd just arrived from the Russian front, and is on his way to America. His hair seemed whiter than before, himself a bit shorter. We ate together, with other American war correspondents. He's exceptionally lively, enthusiastic at finding himself among old friends. He says the Russian soldier is fighting for his country first and foremost, and doesn't care much about communism. A pity the company left me no opportunity to continue this discussion further.

Shepheard's, that caravanserai for all who pass through, has an unlimited monotony about it. Even the monotony of the new face. Every so often you meet someone you last saw in normal or extraordinary circumstances: he's surprised and you're surprised. You ask him, "What happened to you?" and he tells you what he's been doing since then. Then it occurs to you that even these feelings are like a worn suit.

...

Sunday, 6 December

This *idea* of a world that isn't exposed, that isn't boundless, to the extent that you can't see, any more—I dreamed of this last night. I was at Skala,* or rather, I *saw* Skala, because I don't remember that I had the sensation of being there myself, except for the fact that I was looking, longingly, with eyes that must have been as acute as powerful lenses. My vantage point must have been somewhere between our "little house" and

1942

the "steamer jetty." The sea exceptionally calm. Lit by a sun that you could have taken down and placed in your knapsack. Everything: mooring rings on the harbor wall, piles of timber, the arches of the houses, caïques, windows—all of them were *faithful*, in the way we describe a dog as being faithful. And I had the burning conviction that all these things belonged to me, almost that they had been made by my own hands; or that I was a small child and these were my toys.

In the morning, after a round of visits, walking by the Nile, towards Garden City. The ageless shapes of sails; the water rolling by. Sense of horror at the degradation of spirit: you dare not look at it exposed. Sometimes I feel like howling, from frustration at not being able to write.

To Muski. In a shop we looked at cloth and scarabs. The shopkeeper, a Jew from Smyrna, had been here forty years, but still remembered his spoken Greek. My memory retains a piece of red silk picked out in gold, and a little worn green seal, with the engraving of a ship.— "The name of its owner," said the man. What name did he mean?

Later at the castle of Mohammed Ali. The Arabs are expert at separating you from small change, like

Gypsy women at home. Small change to take your shoes before you go into the mosque, small change to turn on the two thousand electric bulbs that light it, small change to show you the view.

We wound up at Shepheard's.

...

Thursday, 24 December

Our second Christmas as exiles. We ate downstairs, just the two of us—in this hotel. In honor of the occasion they'd strung up colored lights, on each table was a yogurt-bowl with wheat or barley seeds that had been soaked for days and were beginning to sprout. Like a distant memory of reed-beds. Down below in the streets, the troops are making mayhem. This morning I noticed for the first time, on a balcony in Sharia Emad-el-Din, where for months now I've been going three or four times a day, an advertising poster: "Hellenic Shipping Ltd." In this street, crammed with troops all at sea in their drunkenness, the abstract notion of the little ships that used to take us once upon a time to the islands of the Aegean: a feeling of great isolation.

1942

Friday, 25 December

What a trial to have to hunt for presents, without enthusiasm and counting every penny. How boring these festivals are. Sometimes I feel I'm going about like the ghost of Hamlet's father, in this camp behind the lines that Cairo has become.* At night the troops hurl empty bottles at passing taxis. The drivers won't risk their vehicles in the busiest streets. Around 11 in the evening the great foyer at Shepheard's full of drunks staggering under the subdued lighting; it's like the salon of a brothel, and the ghost of Hamlet's father, unheard, goes this way and that, crying vengeance.

1943

Sunday, 10 January

In the morning we walked out to the Ibn Tulun Mosque. An old Arab treasure buried in filth, human and literal. The great courtyard with its forty-two doors, empty. The lines of arches changing articulation as you change position: tracery of stone, tracery of wood, tracery of light. We climbed up the minaret of the other mosque, right beside the big one, Sari Ratma: exceptionally clear day with a view as far as the Pyramids. All is well so long as you don't lower your gaze. Once you look down, the wretched tangle of dirty houses and dirty people ruins everything; on the breeze rises a cloud of pulverized camel-dung.

The serious and demanding pose of a little girl singing in the middle of a circle of Arabs. Childhood and youth are non-existent here: either they're babies, or mature adults.

A lazy day today. I needed it. I feel my nerves somewhat more relaxed.

1943

Wednesday, 20 January

At lunchtime, Hasan Fathy. I met him last Sunday at a ceremony to lay a foundation stone, when they took a rusty knife to sacrifice a large coffee-colored lamb. The gaping throat of the beast, where the blood bubbled out, for the rest of the day got mixed up with my left pulse.

We got talking. He told me how the laborers worked at Aswan. The mania of his countrymen to ape Europe makes him very unhappy. I enjoyed his conversation and we agreed that today he'd take me to show me old Arab houses of the fourteenth century.

When he talks, it feels like listening to the muezzin.

Friday, 19 February

Alekos Levides came yesterday, from Athens. He had news of my brother, which confirms what I'd heared from my cousin who in the meantime had got as far as Smyrna. Angelos had had a stomach operation, following a crisis with severe rheumatic pains. The operation had gone well; two ulcers were removed. No sooner was he out of hospital (2 Oct.) than the Italians arrested him (on the 26th) and shut him up for a fortnight in the Averof prison. After that they sent him to Lamia. On 20 November he was allowed to make his way home. It seems they had mistaken him for Alekos Seferiades, who was wanted for resistance activities. I feel sickened by the atmosphere that comes with stories like that. An atmosphere of slavery. We're down so low, without excuse, we're pathetic. I like Levides.

Sunday, 21 February

Early after lunch, to the Pyramids, with Levides. Spring has begun already. Colossal cornerstones in the small temple next to the Sphinx. The stones of Mycenae look like pebbles by comparison. But for all that, I remember them as heavier.

Levides tells me the story of the "Trial of the Accents,"* when Kakrides was taken to court by Exarchopoulos and other self-styled defenders of the Greek language.

Friday, 5 March

Last year, at the end of May and beginning of June, I had invited Larry and Nancy* home for the evening. That afternoon I'd had a typhoid injection. It was the third dose and I was hoping that this time I'd

1943

have no reaction. But as soon as we sat down to table, I was overcome by a fiendish shivering and then an unstoppable raving. Temperature of 40 degrees. They put me to bed. It seems in my delirium I kept telling stories about Ramón Gómez de la Serna,* which I can't imagine that I'd have thought about again since my thirtieth year: the lecture he gave from the back of an elephant in some circus in Paris; the traffic-light he wanted to take home with him, because he felt sorry for it; the society for the preservation of lifeless things. Larry became excited by this performance. Next morning when I was better he telephoned to ask me for details about Ramón.

All this I find again now, along with Katsimbalis* (who appears as "G.K.") and other Durrellian jokers, in "Mythology II"* that he sent me last Saturday with Nanis. I was amused by this poetic traffic; to keep it going I've translated the poem into Greek.

Apart from Katsimbalis and Ramón, all the other proper names of the poem (its "mythological" characters) are translated. As for Karaghiozis,* who is "Marmion" in the original, I'm not entirely responsible: I was following the suggestion of the poet when he answered my query:

". . . As for Marmion, he is the title and chief character of a mediocre heroic poem by Sir Walter Scott—very popular once.

"Anecdote: T.E. Lawrence was discussing the *Iliad* once at Thomas Hardy's lunch-table when the grand old man said 'The *Iliad* is a first-rate poem. First-rate; why, it's in the *Marmion* class.'

"Now how can you translate the reference there? Unless you say men of the Karaghiozi breed!"

Monday, 14 June. Alexandria, Hotel "Windsor"

We've been here since midday last Thursday. We were lucky enough to be given a good room on the fifth floor, right over the sea. After so long, I feel in my element, by accident, suddenly. Maro is pleased. At night, when I lie awake, I hear behind the closed shutters the unending murmur of the waves and the whistling of the wind. I think of all those sleepless nights in Cairo. I associate each bed with a different kind of insomnia. Here it's *pleasant*, if one can say such a thing.

I came here to give a lecture on Palamas, among other things.* The short talk I'd given in Cairo had to be expanded to twice its length. I finished it on Thursday, working on the train, and then here, in the afternoon, having on my left the open window and the view of the Qait Bey fortress, and in the distance convoys of ships going by like phantoms.

That Thursday afternoon brought me back to the state of being human. I mean, without defensive shield and without the reactions of someone going through a wild forest with pistol at the ready. Because that's the way we live in Cairo: it's a jungle or Wild West out of the old films, literally, without exaggeration.

The sea air, and the sails, and the hazy light have made me human again; someone who begins once more to be normally sensitive, I mean without inverted or misplaced sensitivities, who is worthy to raise his head and look at the stars in the sky, without being on his guard—just as he should be.

The prospect of returning to Cairo weighs on me heavily. All I've been through and that noise-ridden hotel come back to me like a nightmare. Let these thoughts be; every road you must follow to the end, since for us there's to be no going back.

...

Sunday, 27 June

At the Botanical Gardens in the morning. We saw not much more than the long, narrow tank with the water-lilies. I don't know their names, none of them was labelled.

Shiny round leaves, some spread out flat on the surface, some curled up, others streaming loose. And the flowers—perhaps *Nymphaea*—white, red, saffron. Strange to observe the *life* in them as they move, like individuals. Another kind of water-lily I haven't seen before, single-leaved, dense, with a stem that sticks up straight, several feet above the water. If you look carefully into this jungle, you can observe *analytically* how they "take off" from the water, just like sea-planes. In the first stage the leaf is as flat as though it's been ironed upon the water; then a swelling begins near the stem, a blister; then the surface of the leaf begins to curl, its contact with the water is reduced, and the stem rises higher. The flowers are either red or white. The bud, more beautiful than the opened flower, is as big as a small pine-cone.

Unbelievable life in this somnolent water. Plants, small fish, birds, and the dragonflies, pale blue the color of wisteria, red with wings as transparent as if they'd been made of cellophane, purple, chasing one another, fighting, mating.

This break from routine brings with it a sudden void, or a sense of time having *mass* and pressing down upon your life, as in "The King of Asine."*

1943

I exercise the profession of human being and the profession of public servant. Things dramatically irreconcilable at times, and sometimes a great weight—and then suddenly, in the blink of an eye, you see yourself without any profession—you see that the one profession cancels out the other.

Sunday, 4 July

Yesterday I was touched to receive a reply from André Gide* to the message I'd sent him last May.

Our world is a tiny grain of sand and in the midst of this dust an eye that can accommodate the universe.

THE ALIBI

He washed his hands
in the waters of the Thames,
in the waters of the Nile,
in the waters of the WC—
he washed his hands
and said, "I'm not the one"
and said, "It isn't me."

Wednesday, 14 July

... In Alexandria I met Henri al-Kayem.* This time last year he'd sent me his poems published by GLM (in the manner of Jouve); but it was only now that we managed to meet. His house is bright, full of light; books with familiar spines. They offer me iced tea and black Havana cigarettes. His wife is as tiny as he is himself: she's a Malgache. Great refinement in the movements of her hands. Both of them very soft-spoken, they almost whisper. In their house I felt crass in my movements, like a steam-roller. There's no peace to spare, to make the most of company like theirs. This time I was sorry for it.

Friday, 23 July

Days of such exhaustion, sometimes I feel as though I've taken my bath in fish-glue. Horrified to find no time left over for thinking: I've turned into a machine.

...

Sunday, 1 August

You ought to leave all this behind—consorting with felons and idiots, helping out—not so as to be able to do something else, or to devote yourself to literature, but to empty your life, to straighten it out.

Thursday, 5 August

> Can it be flat land or maybe
> the bed of a dry sea
> that never will blossom with fish and seaweed;
> where never again will
> the hollow of a keel become
> a shoulder to bear weight
> or, if you prefer, the drawing of a breath—
> We set up theaters and knock them down ...

Saturday, 7 August

On this I insist: why does a certain impression *function* poetically, more than a thousand other daily impressions? Note that it's not the most powerful that is the most effective; very often it's the most slight. No one knows, I suppose. The last time it happened, I was coming down the stairs from the office: I saw a group of carpenters in a room knocking down a stage-set, which had been left over by the previous tenants. I had a feeling like when the camera lens clicks: the impression functioned: why that one and not another? Yesterday I wrote the poem "Mountebanks," never mind whether it's good or not, but why should that have come from *there*?

1943

MOUNTEBANKS, MIDDLE EAST*

We set up theaters and knock them down
every time we come to town—
we set up theaters and stage-sets,
but stronger still are our fates

that sweep away both them and us
mountebanks and impresarios
both the prompter and the band
to every corner of the land.

Flesh and make-up, props and gunny,
rhymes, emotions, costumes, funny
faces, sunsets, wailing, and cries
and loud ejaculations to the skies

thrown along with us into the air
(do *you* know where we're going?—where?)
On our taut skins one observes
like zebra-stripes the naked nerves

naked and light, dry as an oven
(they gave us birth and buried us—when?)
and stretched as tightly as the viol
string that vibrates still. Meanwhile

1943

look into our hearts: a sponge
to hang about bazaars and plunge
down into the blood and grief
of the tetrarch and the common thief.

Middle East, August '43

Τήνεμε θέατρα καί τά χαλνέμε
Όπε σταθέμε κι όπε βρεθέμε
Σίγνεμε θέατρα καί σκηνικά,
Όμως ή μοίρα μας πάντα νικά.

Καί τά ακρώνει καί μας βαρώνει
Καί τίς δεσποίνες καί τό δεσπότη
Πορθλέα καί μουσικές
Στίς πέντε ανέμους τίς βασιλικές.

Σάρκες, κινάιδες, ξύλα, φλασίδια,
Ρίμες, αισθήματα, πέπλα, στοιχίδια,
Μάσκες, χογέρματα, γόοι καί κραυγές
κι' επιφωνήματα καί χαραυγές

Monday, 11 October. [Alexandria, Hotel "Windsor"]

The sea empty, without furniture, like a house with four bare walls. Other times with just one ship, or filled to the horizon with dark shapes. The sea that belongs to no one (a reassuring thing to say), that is as salty as it ought to be (not like the Dead Sea). At night, sometimes, it glows with phosphorescence, like black silk suddenly torn, to reveal a little white flesh. Then the Western Harbor; little craft bustling about like ants, in among the big ships; flags and pennants changing in the sun that strikes a gleam from the aluminum barrage balloons, as they're raised or lowered or moved to different positions, their faces like muzzled sharks.

Ten days of doing nothing, I needed them. Sometimes I'm sorry I couldn't have stayed in Alexandria during all this time of exile, which has driven me to scatter myself to the five winds. I'd have done something; even just with this sea, even just with this harbor. Rivers have no comfort to give you, they need a glad heart; it makes no difference whether it's the Seine, or the Thames, the same too for the Nile. Rivers leave you always behind, as they flow, with what you've got: resentments, troubles, hopelessness. The sea liberates. A person on the riverbank: one of the saddest sights that exist.*

1943

Impossible for me to adjust to any other mythology than the one I've known (since leaving Greece I've come into contact with so many). I kept thinking of this, all the time I was writing whatever came into my head to write about the sea. So these days, too, are gone. Such a strange place is the Middle East, the way it grinds people down, swallows them and digests them. I watch each batch of new arrivals when they come from Greece; they're what they are: human. Give them two weeks, three at most, they start to become *like us*.

1944

Sunday, 26 March

... Last evening I went over A. Xydis's translation of "The Dry Salvages"* with pencil in hand. A terribly difficult text and our language responds to it at times with great resistance. What impresses me, over and over again, is the sound of the voice of this poem; the touch of its voice. It reminds me of the rhythm of the *Canzona*.* It's a rare thing to find such balanced maturity.

Yesterday we lunched at the Peristeria.* On the water a bird shaped liked a hoopoe, with a small fish-colored hump on its back, a beak that makes an almost acute angle with its body. It flies above the current and checks its speed with a play of wings, while it takes its time lining up on the fish. Suddenly it dives into the water, or to just above the surface, so as to rise once more and start again. The Greek waiter calls it a "fish-eater," the Arab *"abu el khut khut"* (Kingfisher).*

Wednesday, 10 May

Since the end of April (the 28th) I've resigned as Director of Press.* The whole month I'd been in it up to here with the Middle East Crisis, much worse than all the others.

...

That's talk for another time. Since the end of April I've felt relieved of the terrible weight of the service that had become as rotten as gangrene. I still have some of the poison in me that I must wash away. This is difficult to do. I've been through a dreadful trial of nerves. I think I kept my head only because, during the few hours I had at home, hours of sleeplessness, I could devote myself to artisan work: copying out the poems of *Logbook II* in manuscript for photographic reproduction with sketches and artwork. It remains a psychological mystery to me—and perhaps it always will—how I was able to do this thing. Searching my memory, I can find only one other case, in the summer of '41 when, on the ship to South Africa, I shut myself in that wretched cabin without a porthole and wrote up my diary, on a fever-hot glass-topped table, as we passed through the tropical heat of the Red Sea. A defense mechanism of the organism, perhaps, against disgust, then as now, and now something else that has reinforced this mechanism, I think: the fact that I can't draw. When I did those pictures, I ought to have put down on paper every possible line and then picked out the one that was right, and rubbed out the others. Perhaps it was this remission, this trusting to the unknown, this walking in darkness, that John of the Cross* had in mind, and that calmed my nerves like a bath.

Inter ceteris, yesterday I received a letter from Timos* who all through the political crisis has been bombarding me with his attempts to translate Eliot's *Sweeney* ("Under the bamboo . . .").* He'd heard what had happened to me, he said, but never mind—happily there is literature and let us return to that. This aestheticism of the ivory tower*—literature as opiate or masturbation, which gets on my nerves and makes me react, sometimes rashly, against my Alexandrian friends, who are such good people in all other respects.

Anyway, Timos wants me to return to literature and write a prologue and a study of the poet for a book that's been commissioned by an Alexandrian publisher, with the title *The Age of Eliot*. My response, which is to send them to the devil, is strong: *The Age of Eliot*, after everything that's been done before our eyes these last few months?* And yet at the same time, to vent my feelings, I've a great desire to concoct an essay in which I'd say: "The time has come to think again about 'The Waste Land.'" I wrote back to Timos asking him to tell me how much the publisher is paying his contributors. That, too, was a form of reaction.

1944

Monday, 21 August [Cairo, 31 Sharia Emad-el-Din]

Sometimes it wears me out, not being able to shut myself up in my lair: deep down, in the midst of all the others, I'm a wild creature. I must make up my mind to it. By choosing the road we have—staying on in Cairo, then going with the first batch to Greece—we've committed ourselves to the hardest course of all. Never mind; the experience of exile we must see through to its end.

Towards evening we went out walking by the Nile, for an hour or so. The river is high and the current terrifically strong below the bridges; you can see whirlpools spinning. Palm-trees against the darkening sky with this exceptionally soft swaying that dances in your mind and truly moves you. The typical colors that presage the night, rose-pink and green.

Monday, 28 August

This morning, at the Ministry, I'm told the decision's been rescinded: I'm being sent to Beirut.

...

Wednesday, 30 August

This morning, at the Ministry. Rescinded again: I'm not going to Beirut, I'm going to Italy. Disgust at the inconsistency of the Service; you feel like howling with rage; what holds you back is the endless emptiness that surrounds you. I told them I'd give my answer by the afternoon. When afternoon comes I give way to Maro's desperation to see her children again, and my own longing to return as soon as possible to my country and draw a line under this nightmare of exile. We're going to Italy, we'll spend wretched times with that crowd; we haven't chosen the easiest road, but God grant it may still turn out the swiftest that leads to home.

Friday, 1 September

Since yesterday we've begun packing up the house. Maro is fixing the trunks. Even though we've had instructions from the British Embassy to be ready on Wednesday the 6th of the month, now they tell us we're leaving today, Friday, at 8. In the meantime the fever of departure has raised a terrific uproar; a dust-cloud of people trying to see where they can attach themselves to gain some advantage.

Now that the days here are running out, I look at Cairo for the first time with sympathy. The great river, as I cross over the bridge, moves me; I'm moved by those great white sails that appear behind the green strips at the side of the roads in Zamalek, like fantastic trees planted in an unsuspected park.

1944

Tuesday, 5 September

All these days undoing the house around us, trunks and suitcases. Maro is literally done in.

Entirely by chance, at 12:00, I'm told that everything not required in cabins must be handed in at the Foreign Ministry by 14:30! Rush home by taxi.

...

I'm in correspondence with Timos about the printing of *Logbook II.** I'm trying to arrange to go to Alexandria and embark from there.

Wednesday, 6 September

I've been given instructions for our departure for Italy: men to be at Cairo railway station by 21:00 on Friday, women at the same place by Saturday noon. Our own services that are supposed to be handling these arrangements have left everything to the mercy of the British, with not a single initiative taken. The scrum of passengers for Naples has been swelled by people that nobody can tell you any possible reason for dragging along. All this reminds me of the exodus from Athens, in '41, or the exodus towards Jerusalem, in '42. And to think that this time it's the exodus for our return in triumph! A shame.

I've asked Frantzis, our amateur liaison-officer, to explain to the British Embassy that I'll be in Alexandria on business in any case, and can they please release me from the bizarre obligation of coming back to Cairo, for no other reason than to join with the others for the journey to Alexandria? I pass the same message through another friend. Frantzis is bored; he puts things off from morning till afternoon, from afternoon till the next morning.

Thursday, 7 September

Frantzis can't get an answer for me. Telephone calls. All day yesterday we had a carpenter so we could be finished with the trunks that have gone today to Alexandria and which I'm leaving for Nikos Pantelidis to send on to me some day. The only thing that I'll treasure from this adventure: a few friends who have shown me touching devotion. At 13:00 Frantzis at last reports: the British Embassy has agreed. We decide to set out at 20:30 by train, the "Diesel" it's called. We were worn out, Maro especially.

Friday, 8 September

Arrived at Alexandria, 01:00, staying with Chronis. Terribly humid, but I'm pleased to have come here, and to have postponed for a short while our immersion in the crowd bound for Naples. Nanis, Timos.* I'm glad I can shake hands with them before leaving. Nanis, who has no idea, as usual, says:

"You ought to go on board now, and choose a nice cabin. Leave your things there, then you can embark at your leisure, at the last moment."

No matter how hard I've tried to explain to him, he still maintains the same unbelievable naïveté about the life we lead. He thinks we're normal people.

Spent the evening at the Excelsior with Nanis and Timos. I was reminded of that other evening, which seems such a long time ago now: we were sitting in the same place. Timos was reading from his notes on Cavafy, when suddenly behind our backs an anti-aircraft battery opened up and gave us the fright of our lives.

Tomorrow we embark.

Saturday, 9 September. SS "Durban Castle"

In the morning I was informed by the officer I was told to ask that we must be at the railway station at 16:20. Time to face up to it: now we're going to be swallowed up by the crowd.

...

The ship is an enormous barracks full to the gunwales (3,500 people, I'm told). No comparison even with the ship that took us from Crete to Port Said, even though this one is bigger and was a luxury liner in its day.

Monday, 11 September. SS "Durban Castle"

A few moments after opening my eyes, at 06:00, I saw the yellow roof that's visible from our porthole begin to move; we're on our way. Sense of heading into the unknown, just like when we sailed from Crete. I went up on deck; Alexandria is leaving;* a strange friendship it's been, between me and this city. Soon the houses along the low harbor wall were lost behind a forest of masts. Alexandria has turned into a ship.

All day unable even to read. The cabin is a good one, only the lack of water is a nuisance. Killing time.

...

Before turning in at night, on deck. Sky with a host of stars and always the majesty of Scorpio with its violet heart, Antares: *Cor Scorpionis*.* This constellation has been following me (or I have been following it) ever since South Africa. I ought to write something with the title: Beneath the Constellation Scorpio.

1944

LAST STOP*

Few are the moonlit nights that have pleased me.
The stars write their own alphabet which you spell out
in the fatigue brought on when the day's tasks are done
and there you can find other meanings, other hopes,
clearer, by far, to read.
Now that I sit idle, recollecting
not many moons remain in memory;
islands the color of a weeping Virgin, late in the waning
or moonlight over northern cities, casting sometimes
on troubled streets and rivers, limbs of people
a heavy lethargy.
And yet, last evening here, in this our last landfall
where we long for the day of our return to dawn
like an old debt, currency that has remained for years
in a miser's chest until at last
the time of reckoning has come and coins
chink tumbling onto the table;
in this Tyrrhenian village, tucked above Salerno and
    the sea
above the harbors of return, the cusp
of an autumn downpour brought the moon
out from behind the clouds, and then
the houses on the farther slope were all enamel.

1944

Beloved silences of the moon.
That, too, is a train of thought, a manner
in which you can begin to speak of things that are
    confessed
with difficulty, at moments when endurance fails, to a
    friend
who has escaped in secret and brings you
news from home and from your comrades,
and you cannot wait to open your heart
before your exiled state pre-empts you, and he too starts
    to change.
We come from Arab lands, from Egypt, Palestine, and
    Syria;
the little state
of Commagene, snuffed out like a small lantern,
is often in our thoughts,
and mighty cities that endured for millennia
only to become grazing ground for water-buffaloes
and fields for sugar-cane and maize.
We come from desert sands and from the seas of
    Proteus
our souls wrung out by public sins,
each one clutching rank or title like a songbird in a
    cage.
The rainy autumn in this hollow of the hills

1944

makes fester in the wounds of each of us
either what you might have called nemesis or fate,
or just bad habits, deceit and guile,
or even selfishness, to benefit from others' blood.
Humankind is easily worn down in wars;
humankind is tender, a sheaf of grass;
lips and fingers yearning for a white breast
eyes half-closed against the glare of day
and legs that would run, even exhausted as they are,
at the slightest whiff of gain.
Humankind is tender and thirsty as the grass,
insatiable like the grass, its nerves are roots that spread;
come harvest-time
let sickles be whetted in the neighboring field;
come harvest-time
some shout to exorcise the demon,
some lose themselves among their wares, and some
    orate.
But exorcisms, wares, orations,
when the living are not there, what good are they?
Can humankind be something different?
Is it not that which transmits life?
A time to sow, a time to reap.

The same things and the same again, you'll tell me,
    friend.

1944

And yet: the way an exile thinks, the way a captive
 thinks, the way
a man thinks when he has become a piece of
 merchandise
cannot be changed, however hard you try.
He might perhaps have wished to stay a king of cannibals
expending his strength on things that no one buys,
to stroll among the agapanthus fields
and hear the tom-toms under the bamboo trees,
his courtiers capering with gigantic masks.
And yet the country they hack and set alight like pine,
 and you see it
whether in the darkened railway carriage, without
 water, windows broken, night after night
or whether in the blazing ship that soon will sink,
 according to statistics,
these things are rooted in the brain and do not change
these things have nurtured images the way that certain
 trees
thrust out their shoots in virgin forests
and spear the ground and so begin to grow again;
they thrust out shoots and grow again traversing
leagues and leagues;
a virgin forest of friends killed is each man's mind.
And if I speak to you in fairy-tales and riddles

1944

it is because they're sweeter in the hearing, and the
    horror
cannot be spoken of because it is alive
because it is unspeakable and goes forward;
dripping by day, dripping into sleep
the *pain-perpetuating memory of pain.*

Let me speak of heroes, let me speak of heroes: of
    Michael
who fled the hospital with open wounds
perhaps he spoke of heroes when, that night
dragging his leg across the blacked-out city,
he touched the pain of us all and howled: "In darkness
we go forward, in darkness we go forward . . ."
Heroes go forward in the dark.

Few are the moonlit nights that have pleased me.

Cava dei Tirreni, 5 October '44

PART II

THE PASSING OF EMPIRE (1953–1956)

With "Last Stop" the first "chapter" of Seferis's travels in the Levant comes to a close. On his return to Greece, at the end of the three-and-a-half-year German occupation, Seferis served for a year and a half as political secretary to Archbishop Damaskinos, the country's regent, or temporary head of state. The diaries for the 1950s on several occasions recall this period, when Seferis carried a serious degree of political responsibility and was often required to act as high-level emissary between the British ambassador, Rex Leeper, and the highest levels of the Greek government. It was during this period, too, when Seferis accompanied the regent on an official visit to London in 1945, that a request was first made to the British government to cede the island of Cyprus, with its 80 percent Greek Orthodox population, to Greece. Nothing came of that initiative, of which Seferis himself may have been the instigator, but the memory would add poignancy to Seferis's experience of British colonial intransigence in Cyprus when he visited the island in the 1950s.

During the second half of the 1940s, Greece was torn apart by a vicious civil war between Communist guerrillas and the royalist government, backed first by Britain and then, from 1947, by the United States. The government won, and Greece was secured for the Western bloc in the division of Europe between Western capitalism and Eastern communism that would last for half a century.

As these events were going on, Seferis found himself serving as first secretary in the Greek Embassy in the Turkish capital, Ankara. While there, he spent all the time that he could spare exploring the remains of the Greek, Byzantine, and Ottoman civilizations that had successively left their mark on the Anatolian landscape. He also made a memorable excursion back to his birthplace, Smyrna, and to the seaside village of Skala, where he had spent the happiest times of his life, his childhood summers up to the age of twelve. GS's journals for this period appeared in translation as A Poet's Journal: Days of 1945–1951 *(see notes to pages xiii, 67).*

At the beginning of the 1950s, a diplomatic posting to London brought Seferis into contact with the British literary elite, including T.S. Eliot, whose work he had admired for twenty years and whom he now met for the first time. This was the period when Seferis's international reputation as a poet became securely established. To his pre-war collections of poetry, three volumes had now been added: Logbook II, *the fruit of his years in exile during World War II; the long, dense, complex meditation on the aftermath of war, published in 1947 with the title* "Thrush"; *and a first volume of essays.*

At the end of 1952, Seferis found himself promoted to ambassadorial rank and entrusted with a roving mission to Lebanon, Syria, Jordan, and Iraq. His base was to be Beirut, and he was also accredited by his government to the Orthodox Patriarchate of Jerusalem. (At that time the Patriarchate, in the Old City of Jerusalem, fell within the territory of Jordan.) Given the sensitivities of the time, there was no question of him travelling to Israel. The states to which he found himself accredited had all quite recently become independent after several decades of rule through Western "mandates"; the longest-established was Iraq (independent since 1937).

During the following four years, Seferis travelled all over the region. He also, in November 1953, made the first of three private visits to Cyprus, then a British crown colony and in the grip of a growing political momentum, among its Greek Orthodox population, for self-determination, which in this case meant union (Enosis) *with Greece. Seferis fell in love with the island during this series of visits. At the end of 1955 he published a volume of poems, now known by the title* Logbook III, *largely inspired by his experiences there and dedicated "to the people of Cyprus, in memory and love."*

It was also while he was living in Beirut, and under the influence of his recent experience of Cyprus, that Seferis wrote his only completed work of fiction. Throughout the first half of 1954 he worked at a white heat, revising his personal diaries and an earlier draft from the late 1920s, to produce Six Nights on the Acropolis, *a flawed but remarkable novel that would not see the light of day until after his death, and is only now about to appear in English translation.* The entries relating to this in the* Levant Journal *are among the few in all of Seferis's diaries that reflect directly upon his experience of the creative process.*

A Levant Journal *ends with Seferis's farewell round of visits in 1956, preparatory to leaving his post and returning to Athens, where he would soon become embroiled at first hand in the tense diplomatic negotiations that would eventually lead to the creation of the independent Republic of Cyprus in 1960. Flying over the desert, and unable to land in Baghdad because of a summer dust-storm, Seferis occupies himself with reading the letters of Gertrude Bell, written from those same regions during World War I, and he speculates bitterly on how little has been learnt by Bell's countrymen of her own heartfelt response to that part of the world and its peoples.*

Thereafter Seferis's diplomatic career reached its peak with his posting to London as ambassador from 1957 to 1962; a year after that, the seal was set on his international reputation as a poet with the Nobel Prize for Literature. His last major work to be published during his lifetime was Three Secret Poems, *which appeared in 1966. In April 1967, a military coup ushered in seven years of dictatorship in Greece. After a period of self-imposed silence, the elderly and by this time ailing Seferis took the courageous step of broadcasting a defiant message, via the BBC Greek Service, condemning the imposition of censorship and the abolition of freedom in his country. This act, more than anything he did in his long diplomatic career, ensured him a place in the hearts of his country's youth—that, and the much-loved musical settings of some of his poems by the popular composer Mikis Theodorakis, many of which are still "classics" in Greece today, and have been heard around the world.*

Seferis died in September 1971, and his funeral was turned into one of the few spontaneous, and bloodless, mass demonstrations against the regime.

R.B.

1953

Saturday, 18 April [on the road to Baghdad]

> There is no landlord to the desert
> The desert is a sea
> Largely cocacola-ized countries.
> Charm of desert it is not a desert a wilderness
> Euphrates then the Mesopotamia

H4 a kind [of] approach to a country club somehow puritan (for example no mirrors in the bedroom) but the kind [where] one wouldn't be astonished to see an old gentleman eating his dinner with his bowler hat on.*

Saturday, 4 July. Damascus

In the afternoon I visited the grave of Ianthe.* It's in the Protestant cemetery; a small, untended rectangular space, behind a rusty gate. The custodian knew the name, and showed us, far down on the left, the long, narrow, low gravestone with the cross carved in relief. I copied down the English epitaph.

...

It was getting dark, a wind was blowing. Between the grave and the surrounding wall was a great walnut tree heavy with ripening fruit. Around it were three fig trees, odd how they grew beneath its great shadow. The only growing things in this desert landscape. You felt relief at this gift of fate to the woman who so loved gardens. Night had already deeply stained the breeze that came and went through the branches. Little by little the foliage became the cool mouth of a black cave whose exit you cannot guess. And this movement—of the breeze and the leaves—made you feel that the long, narrow body of Ianthe, turned to marble and transfigured, was journeying above the abyss, the scent of the walnut tree, with the hopeless longing of that tree.

Sunday, 5 July. Beirut. Evening

I haven't been able to rid myself of the astonishing shadow of that tree yesterday.

Thursday, 20 August

Waves from the depths of misery breaking sometimes on the surface.

Saturday, 5 September

The treadmill of my public life shows no signs of letting up—nor does the exhaustion or the sense of shame that are the price of our daily bread. One good thing comes out of this torment: it hasn't assimilated me: I'm not like the foods it habitually digests. As a man of letters I belong to a world that it shuts out; as a man without means, the same; the same, too, as a man with decent reactions, and with the conscience of one who serves. All these things will not change; let them at least leave God out of it.

Friday, 25 September

With Alekos Xydis*—he's been staying with us since yesterday, on his way to Australia—at the Cave of Adonis. A deep cleft, a bottomless cave. Survival of the ancient worship at the foot of the temple of Aphrodite: the Virgin Mary in an alcove, rags hung up as offerings in the branches of an aged fig-tree near her icon. The best of the moderns in a worn piece of graffiti below the table where we sat to eat, as though out of nowhere: "Here was inspired one of the most beautiful chapters of the work of Barrès."* The villager (a Muslim) who exploits the visitor here knows his way round the channels of the cave. He says: "*King* Adonis spends his summers here, in winter he goes down to Byblos." That's all he knows. The water doesn't come out through the cave, the way it looks in photographs, but further down. Full of apples, the country round here.

One can *imagine* how suggestive this place could be; at the moment it's like material for a composition that has to be assembled with effort; perhaps it's the fault of the season, a dry one. Still, the great womb of the cave is there.

Saturday, 26 September

To Sidon, about 11:00. Heavy, humid heat. Much filth; these people urinate everywhere. Better not to see this place, if you've a mind to ponder Cavafy's perfumed youths.* We went up the mountain to find the grave of Hester Stanhope.* At Djoun they could tell us nothing and we turned to the Monastery of the Savior (the monks are Melchites–Uniates*) for information. A large monastery, with a seminary. A priest with an enormous belly and the tall cap of the Orthodox said to us with condescending irony, in French: "So you seek the sorceress of Djoun,"* and pointed to the hillside opposite.

"She was a crazy one . . . She used to say that Christ is coming, no matter what. She had two mares, a tawny one and a white one, and she was waiting for Christ to descend upon one or the other." (In the tone of a man who's become the victim of unfair competition.)

"Did she do good for the people here?" I asked.

"What good could she do?" he replied, as though I'd asked something wildly improbable. "A lot of foreigners came to see her. Among them Lamartine."

"It was here that Lamartine wrote his poem 'Le coucher du soleil,' " put in another monk.

"She used to torture her servants. You can still see the basement where she confined them and tortured them. You'll see it when you go."

"And her grave is there?"

Condescension again. "It used to be nothing. The grave of a simple villager. It was we who took care of it."

What a dangerous thing it can be, at times, to have a vision of Christ!

Sunday, 27 September

Australia, that Xydis is on his way to discover, prompts the thought: how little I'm attracted by the antipodes: those places that remind you the earth is a sphere. I remember, in South Africa, being repelled by the exotic fruit with unknown names. I feel much more at home with the Homeric conception of the earth as a flat disk; places on its surface that allow you to think you can reach out and touch them with your hand. Deep down, I must be incurably old-fashioned.

Tuesday, 6 October. Amman. Hotel "Philadelphia"

Left Beirut yesterday at 07:30. At 09:30, meeting at the Foreign Ministry in Damascus. Lunch here at 14:30. You try to find something pleasant about this desert you're passing through. Nothing but camels; sometimes in the distance they look like tortoises on stilts. Everything else a horror: houses and people—an exception perhaps the outline of a woman going along with a pitcher on her head. Amman—a village with modern trimmings, built at the bottom of a hole—I don't want to say repellent. The only saving grace is the great shell of the ancient theater opposite the hotel where we went out walking—when you come close, it's a latrine—everywhere is filthy. To work in these parts you need the protection of a home—the meanness of public service compels you to wander, exposed. It's a question whether Greece is capable of exercising a policy of influence, a policy in distant places. What can an accountant understand of missions such as mine?*

1953

Wednesday, 7 October. Amman

These Arab cities. Half permanent, half nomadic. Houses half buildings, half encampments. The horror of civilization chipping away all round you like a chisel, and all you can feel are the splinters. This pitiable dust in your eye: coca-cola-ism, pepsi-cola-ism.* Cars handled like drunken camels, and the ancient monuments, ancient beyond hope, mixed up in this inhuman muddle—sometimes it seems a pathetic nightmare.

Yesterday at the house of the doctor, the honorary consul. His wife is French, he's very well off—with a mania for travelling the world by airplane. It could have been the ante-chamber of a modern *Inferno*. Photographs on the wall: the Bedouin father, face like a bird of prey or *Pelecanus onocrotalus*,* wife at his side wearing a large cross. They're Orthodox Christians—bare electric bulbs—lacework made of nylon—a colossal *frigidaire* in the dining-room: Hostile walls, my God! I'm tired.

...

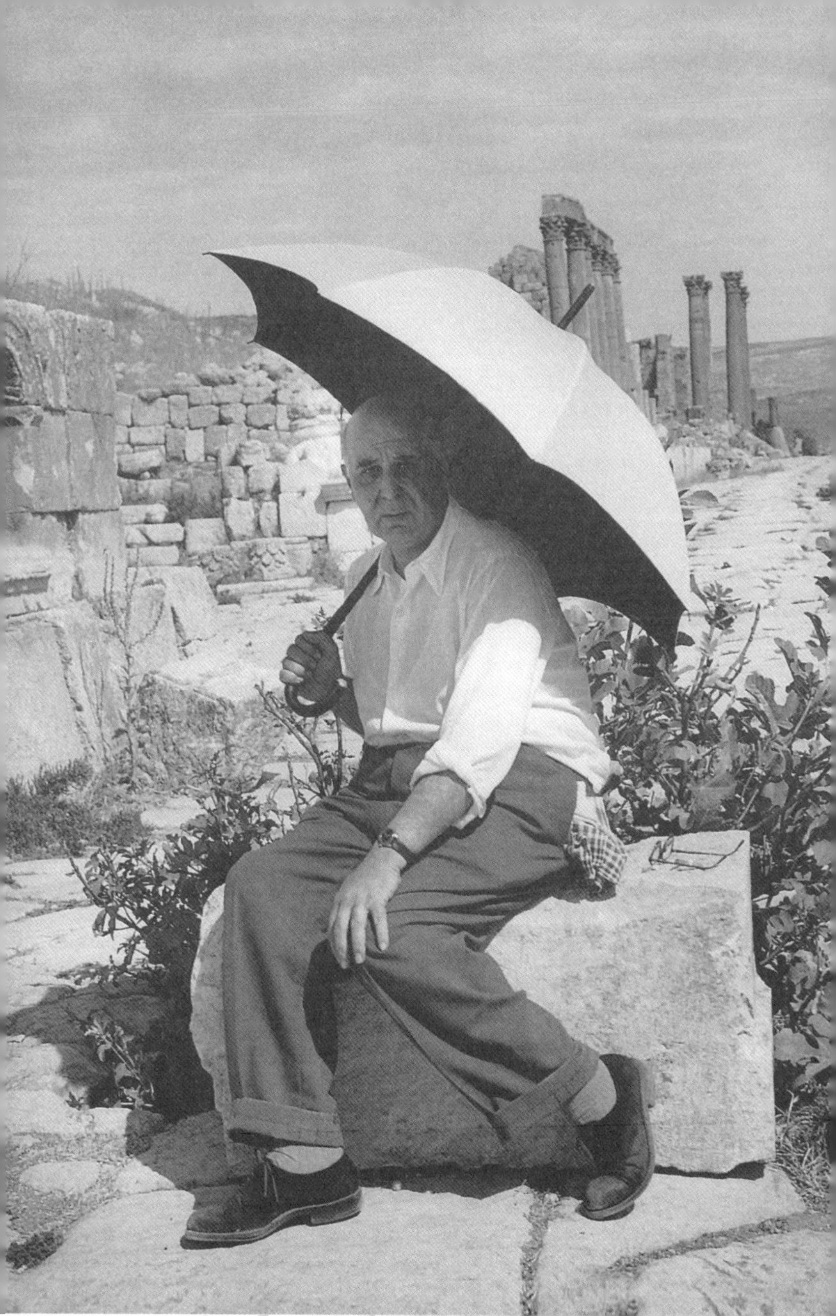

1953

Saturday, 10 October. Jerusalem

Sudden sense of hurt. The other afternoon, looking out over the hills of Jerusalem, this need to soothe the hurt. Such a great need.

In the morning at the Mosque of Omar. Afternoon at the site of the Ascension, an octagonal old Byzantine building that inspired the idea of the mosque. The rock with the imprint of Christ's foot. Then, up at the Patriarch's villa, the Lesser Galilean. Wonderful sunset. Such need, such need for these things: here you can breathe—why does this not happen in Lebanon?

Sergeya the nun: she paints, at over 70. She paints, she runs ahead of us like a little gazelle, takes her cheeks in both hands and says, "I haven't grown old." (She's Russian.) As we're leaving, she says to us, "May the Angel go with you!"

Seraphim, the Russian monk, like a character out of Dostoyevsky.

The panorama of Jerusalem, evening in the garden—the Mount of Olives.

Thursday, 5 November

> *I begin to think that people in government posts*
> *Get no rest, except by falling ill!*
>
> Po Chü-i (772–846 A.D.)*

1953

Friday, 6 November ... Nicosia. Hotel "Ledra Palace"

My first time in Cyprus. (I don't count the two hours spent ashore last December in Limassol, where the ship put in on the way to Beirut.)

I mean to note down my impressions as they come to me, unchecked; no clever tricks; like twitches of the needle, I'll see later where it comes to rest.

First impression: from here one feels Greece (suddenly) to be more spacious, broader. The sense that there exists a world of people speaking Greek, a Greek world. One that doesn't depend on the Greek government, and this last contributes to that sense of spaciousness.

Question: Are we worthy to administer Cyprus, and not do harm to that world, trying to make it better, without turning it into a province of the Greek mainland, like Corfu, like Salonica?*

The journey by airplane from Beirut was quick and easy; it lasted an hour. At the airfield was the Consul General of Greece with his wife—and Evangelos Louizos and Maurice Cardiff.*

On the part of Greek officialdom: they're terrified in case I overstep the mark, especially with the British (they needn't be; I know very well what I'm going to do). On the British side: spontaneous signs of friendship certainly (I've known Cardiff for eight years now). But the most unpleasant thing is that these spontaneous signs of friendship, *here*, you can't judge as though you were an independent human being: you can't separate them from the political tinge they acquire, or from the official position that any British friend from before has to take up here, or from the anti-British attitude of the Cypriots. Very unpleasant.

In the evening we went out with Evangelos Louizos into the streets of Nicosia. It was already dark. Gothic buildings, fortification walls, the courtyard of the Great Han. Fine architecture. Narrow streets with few passers-by. Not like the Middle East. More of a Mediterranean feel. Here and there in the alleyways, open doorways revealing lighted, narrow, humble interiors: miniature brothels. The whole place seems dripping with sensuality.

Some tiredness still. I'm glad to have left Beirut. Feeling that by a hairsbreadth I've escaped from a trap in which I was well and truly caught.

Saturday, 7 November

In the morning official visits, signing the Governor's book. Then at the Archbishop's Palace, to see the Ethnarch.* I spent a couple of hours with him. Then with my diplomatic colleague here, who delivers himself of many compliments and a fair amount of drivel.

The Cyprus issue:

(a) I don't believe the Ministry in Athens has hit upon a line that it intends to follow through with vigor. They're biding their time: having it both ways. The issue is tricky: it resides at a level far above the intellectual or executive capabilities of the run-of-the-mill civil servant. At this high level, I can think of no one up to the job.

(b) From the point of view of the way the service is organized here: the usual meanness of spirit. A consul general and two assistants. That's a staff to cope with routine business and maintain contact with the Archbishop. But that way, and given the mentality of the people who have served here (I can think of a succession of them over some fifteen years), you don't nurture and you certainly don't influence a population of 400,000. Here as everywhere else, mean-minded economies: with this kind of meanness you don't threaten an empire.

(c) The most important thing to come out of talking to the Archbishop is that something has to happen soon. Because the Ethnarchy, try as it might, can't keep popular sentiment on its side forever: it's afraid that if a solution is postponed we could find ourselves in the very unpleasant situation where we might lose a referendum if it took place in 2-3 years' time. Naturally, the British know this and make the most of it.

...

Friday, 13 November

Morning: Agianapa. The great sycamore tree. A hero among trees.

> *Beneath the sycamore tree . . .**

Afternoon: to Engomi, to see the excavations on the plain. Astonishing afternoon; the site of a Mycenaean city, immobilized for thousands of years. Roads, houses with their foundations marking out the shape of a life that has ceased—a stagnant power, and further down this way, more strongly, where the foundations of the fortifications show through, mighty stones laid out like the petrified muscles of Titans. The light was dancing and not dancing; the blue of the sky gives you the feeling of a love unborn, inconceivable and yet there. Infinite curlicues of clouds and here and there the red-gold of a flaring trumpet. The flatness of the plain like an offering, and in the palm of this great hand lies the ancient city, the lines of fate frozen into immobility.

There must have been something in all this that caught you by the throat.

1953

The girls—dancing—you saw them as though naked. One in particular.

ENGOMI*

Give life to the clouds if you can
give to the boundless silence speech
like the god's embrace is this open plain
the light is dancing and not dancing
the girl's breast firm and tender
points to the lips of an unknown infant.

At the time of the equinox a little afterwards

I sought here in this place respite
from the sand of the desert.
...

Sunday, 6 December

... At the dervish *tekke*.* Floor; chairs behind—two Turkish officers—schoolgirls; infants, making a fair amount of noise—two old men and five young ones in the tall cinnamon-colored fez—up on the balcony three musicians—all dressed the same, in black cassocks. They stood on the left; then the oldest of them came in wearing a green turban wound round his fez; the singing began, they went once or twice round the chamber bowing down before the sheikh and each one turning and bowing to his fellow; they did this two or three times, then with eyes closed and arms spread wide in the air they began to revolve, as though entering a different element, the old man in their midst—then the other old man, and third the sheikh, they danced without their cassocks, white robes beneath, open to the air—at the start they'd taken off their shoes—the sheikh at the beginning on his knees invoked the Turkish Republic and Mustafa Kemal Pasha.* At the end they cried "Oo! Oo! Oo! Oo!"

Who has ever thought to ask, how can we find a substitute for things like this?

1954

*Monday, 11 January, Beirut**

Saturday and Sunday without a break, in my study copying out the *Acropolis** for the journal of 1927–1929. I'm impressed at the way memory effortlessly fills out those manuscripts—such an effort to write them *then*—like copying from a text that already exists. Idea this morning: to let memory do its work—*retrospectively* to add to the old manuscript—to complete it. I was particularly struck by the Refutation of FIRE in Pascal's "Mémorial." I hadn't noticed it then (strangely enough: how could something so important have escaped me? it's a basis, even)—at bottom what's remarkable is the link between sensuality and deprivation of place that comes with the place—something that I encountered later in Cairo, when I said to a friend, *"La guerre nous mange le sexe."** I must, if I decide to go on with this, and the strange thing is that I've a great relish for this thing. Strange that the sensual aspect should have escaped me then; this is what I'm going to add in the rewriting. I think:

(a) I ought to avoid *anything weighty*, or pressure, as I'm in the habit of doing when I write—leave memory alone to function automatically—this is the new idea that's attracted me so much today—the pen gliding over the paper. I must carry on like this.

3rd person.

Tuesday, 19 January. 6:30 AM

I awoke refreshed, outside it's still dark. Out at sea, a lot of ships, all lit up, waiting to enter the port. I feel refreshed, sitting at my work table.

Dream, which I can't explain (usually I do explain them, or rather I can recognize their ingredients). I'm talking with Churchill in London, not in an enclosed space but not outdoors either. There's a third man with us, maybe Katsimbalis. I'm asking Churchill about his life, and he's answering (I don't remember the details). Finally, the conversation comes round and he's speaking in Greek and quoting Venizelos,* words spoken by Venizelos, conscripted to serve as a historic proclamation—the two of us resented this and began to cry: he's behaving just like us.

For ten days now, an orgasm of writing. In a dream-like state, seeing visions, nothing touches me, I can't turn aside to attend to my day job. I was thinking that this way I'll leave the drudgery behind, not because of some decision, but insensibly, being so much caught up in the true life.

Saturday

If only one could imagine what I'm going through, writing the *Acropolis*.

Driving power—tremendous.*

Dear God—to write is a beautiful thing, but not to be able to return to the daily routine . . .

Monday, 22 February

After lunch to Djoun, to see the house of Lady Hester Stanhope.* Her grave without a cross: a cube at the top of three steps: "Lady Hester Lucy Stanhope, born 12th March 1776, died 23rd June 1839."* And the ruined houses inhabited by the villagers. In her bedroom on the right is a blind old man, on the left a woman who looks better off—great storage jars for corn and oil—next door, people and cattle living together.

Spring in these environs of Sidon;* a sunny afternoon—countryside full of olive trees and bright-red anemones, cyclamen.

This strange sensation I feel. I always need a "spiritual hinterland" before I can experience a landscape properly.

1954

Friday, 16 April. Amman*

At the museum the director shows me a find from beneath the floor of a neolithic house in Jericho. It's a skull *supplemented* with plaster (5000 B.C.E.). Into its eye-sockets have been inserted fragments of shells. You wonder, could these be the first fumblings in the direction of sculpture? They start by supplementing nature, then they imitate it.

Madaba. Very close: the excursion can be made in an afternoon to Madaba and Pisgah (Byzantine basilica with mosaics on the floor covered over with earth—mountain where Moses died—needs a day with clear sky for the view, which is splendid). Madaba: Arab Orthodox church with the famous map*—terrible state of neglect—the map covered over with planks. The sacristan has to lift them for you to see it. Sadly, they've built the church without the least concern for the mosaic map. Today even the stalls (on the right, looking towards the altar) are in the way, as they're placed on top of it. Terrible difference when you contemplate the care taken by the Catholics (Terra Santa) over at Pisgah.

...

1954

Saturday, 17 April

At Jerusalem. We've moved into the Patriarchate. A room opposite the refectory. Washing, etc. difficult, because the windows have no shutters and overlook the alley.

...

Vespers for Palm Sunday. My first liturgy at the Holy Sepulchre: "I shall enter into Thy dwelling, O Lord." Great emotion when the accompanying priests sang those words. Stern faces of the guardians of the Sepulchre. The Armenian, the Catholic, and ours. The Armenian looked like a ruffian. The Byzantine expression of the Dragoman. Suddenly in the middle of the ceremony, high up under the dome a sounding block struck up in the rhythm of "the *talanto*,"* louder and louder as it went on:

> The-*ta*, the-*ta*, the-*ta-lanto*
> the-*ta*, the-*ta*, the-*taaa-lanto*

a crazy beat:

> *Otototoi Apo-o-o-o-ollo, Apo-o-o-o-ollo**

1954

Tradition like a wave, stronger than humans themselves, and nothing else has any meaning any more: not the skulduggery and simony of the monks, nor the ironmongery and planks that hold up the church, not even the terrible bad taste that marks every aspect of the ritual.

Beside me, a little old woman. I speak to her. She's from Paphos in Cyprus. It's taken her fifteen days to get here, so she tells me. It may well have taken her fifteen years to scrape together the pennies for the journey.

Tuesday of Holy Week, 20 April

At St. Sabba, the monastery, with Alexis Ladas: "in a dry and thirsty land, where no water is."* Dry hills. The monastery is on the western side of the Dead Sea. The monks, very old, most of them. There was a liturgy going on in the church as we entered, acts of contrition, hugging of icons, caressing them, even. A few of the monks were younger, but even they are of the previous generation: like everywhere else, at the Holy Sepulchre the young aren't interested any more: the way things are going, Greek Orthodoxy isn't going to last much longer in these parts. Still, it's only Byzantium that's alive in this monastery, there's nothing of the Greek state here. A monk (middle-aged) tells me legends and episodes

1954

of history (without distinguishing them); he reminds me of the prophecies of Ptocholeon. He says, "Our emperor Constantine," as though it had been yesterday or as if the last emperor of Byzantium were still alive. He loathes the Latins, with a deadly loathing.

I look at the icons in the church: I examine a few that are good. The monk observes, "In those days they used to fast so as to make icons, not like today." This is Brother Glykerios, from Kastelorizo.

...

Of the monks there, 20 are Greek, 3 Romanian, 3 Russian, and 2 are locals.

Brother Seraphim, the steward of the monastery: women are not allowed to enter.

They gave us to drink from the Communion wine.

Wandering around I saw their food laid out in a corner (everything, kitchen, refectory, very well kept): bread, three small onions (white roots and green above), and an orange.

On Easter Day they eat only fish—meat, never.

As we were leaving the bells began to ring.

The sound was submerged or left hanging forever in the desert.

...

1954

Maundy Thursday

Here one goes to sleep at 9 and wakes up at dawn. The alleyway beneath our window fills up early with pilgrims (this year 1,500 have come from Cyprus): little old women and men in traditional costume, most of them: a bundle over the shoulder, a folding stool and a walking-stick, each day at dawn I hear them striking with those sticks on the paving of the roadway.

According to a monk in the service of the Holy Sepulchre the reason so many of them are old is that after the pilgrimage to the Sepulchre it's a sin to have carnal relations.

In the morning at the dais the washing of the feet; even though the socks and shoes of the priests who represent the disciples are briefly disconcerting, there are moments that make you think of an illuminated manuscript.

Good Friday

The Cypriot men with their baggy knee-length pantaloons; there's an air of youthful vigor about them. I remember Panagiotis in the Municipal Market at Famagusta: "Look at me, I'm the only man about here; all the others are wearing trousers!" Archbishop

1954

Makarios's father (he too wears pantaloons) in the church of St. Constantine.

...

It's damp inside the monastery. I've caught a terrible dose of flu—on the way into church I'm shivering.

Ceremony of the Epitaphios in the evening: a disappointment. Impossible to imagine the human capacity for making a mess of things. Here in these holy places, we've turned the burial of Christ into an excuse for bombast. A sermon on Golgotha by a Greek-American priest, in English; down below a sermon in Arabic, another in Greek outside the Sepulchre. Of course, after the hymn, *Life, in the tomb wast thou laid*, came a short psalm. Sometimes, you think to yourself, it may be better to hear these acts of devotion, rather than see them. Fortunately, there are still the little old women, and the Cypriots.

This morning an old woman (from Greece) died. She was 85. They buried her in the shroud she had worn to be baptized in the Jordan. She had made all the pilgrimages: she'd been to Jericho, had climbed to the Monastery of the Forty Days in the heat of noon. This morning, among all the others who had been accommodated here for Easter, she didn't wake up. The abbot Theodosios (from Bethany), who brought me the news, told it joyfully. All the others, too, experienced this death as though it had been a blessing. I don't know why one might say that it wasn't.

Sunday, 15 August

Today, the Feast of the Assumption, I finished the *Acropolis*. I've worked on it since the beginning of the year like a madman—in waking and in sleeping. I can rarely remember such a thing happening to me before: a few weeks in South Africa and when I was writing "Erotikos logos."* Unbelievable driving power. I slept only four hours a night and felt no tiredness—no small thing in this climate.

Saturday, 16 October [Cyprus]

Morning: bathe in the sea.
Afternoon at Engomi. The archaeologists had gone; the place was deserted, except for the custodian.
Splendid flatness of the plain here, splendid.
I walked for some time following the city walls; a large part of them has been cleared since last year. The great stones eroded. Twilight. Suddenly in front of me a snake, quite a long one (more than the length of my walking-stick), gliding sinuously among the humble

weeds (from right to left, not up and down) with a careless air of confidence—the locals refer to it as a "monster."*

Saturday, 18 December [Beirut]

To Byblos with Despina and Anna*—perhaps the first (at most the second) perfectly beautiful day here. We left around 12. Autumnal sunshine. We went up to Ghazir, thinking we were going to Amshit (to see the house where Renan stayed*). We asked the way; first they showed us the house and then they wanted to know who Renan was. And all the time the sea at our feet (Djouniyé bay). On the way back, we ate beneath a great carob-tree—a little boy was picking carobs while looking after two diminutive dun-colored cows.

Byblos, we made our way round the ancient site. Beautiful light-effects on the façades of the houses beyond, and on the crusader castle. Below, near the Church of St. John, the little harbor.

A Phoenician softness about the sea and shore. A "Western" tenderness.

Harbors of the Crusaders; "chivalry"; the conventional things, in inverted commas—Pre-Raphaelite, something like that.

1954

At Amshit, the grave of Henriette Renan—enclosed in a narrow rectangle. A large oak-tree gave it shade. On the outside a stupid plaque announcing that Barrès too had passed this way. We tried to find the house where Renan* had stayed (it has the name Zakia), a beautiful Lebanese house; the interior, large hall. We were shown the small room where he lived. Mementos were a small travelling cabinet, a letter of his from 19 Sept. '86—his shadow falls heavily here.

We stopped a little way below Amshit and watched the sun sink beneath the calm sea of *Phoenicia*.

But why should it be that sometimes one sees things *clearly*—I mean like when the camera is properly adjusted—*

1955

Sunday, 12 June [Beirut]

Dance. At the end of the day the root of the dance lies in Aphrodite, in the sensual body. In the erotic gyrations of that belly writhing around an invisible penis (like last evening, for example) or in the aroused body on the way to kill or be killed—(which is the same thing). Those things and the way out from those things are the dance. The way out from those things as in the whirling dervishes who seem to glide towards a different element in which they are lost or forget themselves. Between these two extremes, I found myself thinking this morning, lies the dance. And this explains for me why I find ballet so idiotic, with its sterilized bodies, sterilized symbolism, romantic gestures, poses, etc. Rather than ballet, I'd prefer a choreographed pantomime.

Belly rhythmically writhing like a beaten tambourine —hips twitching as if penetrated.

(Tahia Carioca—she dances at the Auberge.)

Sunday, 7 August. Evening

It's time, I suppose, to begin to think of learning how to pray.

1955

In July I took up writing poems again: "Helen," "Engomi," "The Demon of Fornication." "Helen" has been in my mind since last year, "Engomi" since the year before. I mean, from the time when I began to make notes. I was able to write them, after the arid spell that was the first half of this year, because at last I found a week's holiday, during the first days of July, when we went to Bhamdoun.* This event is something I ought to remember. The "Demon" and "In the Kyrenia District" were exercises. Still, those were the most interesting things (those four poems) I've done this year. Those and the frangipani-tree, the cutting I took at Byblos in the spring; Maro planted it and I watched the buds swell slowly until they burst and turned into flowers.

1955

ENGOMI

The plain was broad and level; from a distance could
 be seen
the wheeling arms of people digging.
In the sky the clouds with many curlicues, here and
 there
a trumpet golden and rosy; dusk.
Among the sparse weeds and thorns wandered
light breezes after rain; it must have been raining
over there where the tops of the mountains were taking
 on color.

And I went forward towards the people who labored,
women and men with pick-axes in trenches.
It was an old city; fortifications, streets, and houses
stood out like petrified muscles of giants,
the anatomy of a spent power beneath the eye
of archaeologist, anesthetist, or surgeon.
Phantasms and fabrics, luxury and lips, swallowed up
and the curtains of pain thrown open wide
to reveal naked and indifferent: the grave.

And I looked up towards the people who labored
the stretched shoulders and arms that struck

1955

in a rapid and heavy rhythm at this dead thing
as though the wheel of fate were passing over those ruins.

Suddenly I was walking and not walking
I was watching the birds in flight, and they were turned
    to marble
I was watching the brightness of the sky, and it was
    dimmed
I was watching the bodies' effort, and they were stilled
and in their midst a figure rising, riding the light.
Hair black and loose to the shoulders, eyebrows
arched above the lips, then the torso
emerging from the throes of labor stripped naked
with the unripe breasts of the Virgin,
dance without movement.

And I lowered my eyes to look around me:
girls were kneading, and touched no dough
women were spinning, and no spindle turned
lambs were drinking, and their tongues were still
above green water that seemed lulled into sleep
and the plowman had stopped, his goad mid-air.
And again I looked at that body rising;
many had gathered, like ants,
and struck at her with lances but did not wound her.

1955

Now her belly shone like the moon
and I believed that the sky was the womb
that had given her birth and was taking her back,
    mother and child.
Her legs remained marble still
and disappeared: an Ascension.
                              The world
was becoming again what it had been, our own
with time and earth.
                    Scents of lentisk
began to stir upon old hillsides of memory
bosoms among foliage, moistened lips;
and everything became dry at once in the flatness of
    the plain
in the stone's despair the eroded power
in the empty land of sparse weeds and thorns
where carefree on its way a snake glides by,
and where much time is taken up with dying.

1956

Sunday, 4 March. "American Colony" [Jerusalem]

From the window of the hotel room (no. 3, facing north), in the foreground pine-trees—on the left the little minaret and its muezzin; on the high ground in the distance the flags of the consulates. The Turkish on the left—then the French, the Belgian. Heavy rain all these days and fairly cold—today the sun is shining. Bored to death with one-sided, nationalistic posturing, which seems to me increasingly suspect too. Impression that they could condemn you to death and still smile at you just like that.

Friday morning the bombshell burst: Glubb Pasha* has been thrown out of Jordan. It was spectacular—panic among the foreigners. They put him on an airplane and packed him off as a present to the British (Eden)—and Coghill* with him (the brother of Neville); he was in Jericho that night, at the "Sugar Mill," with Stewart Perowne, when the expulsion order came. According to Amman radio, there are mobs demonstrating their gratitude in the streets. "British have been taken by surprise,"* says the General. Stewart Perowne was here on Friday afternoon briefly, from Jericho; tense and cagey: "Rain is not good for politics."* Freya Stark,* the writer, short and plump with very fat ankles. When she answers you, it's as though she's hearing voices: "One writes wherever one happens to be, it would be the same even in Paradise."

...

We entered Amman a little after midday. We got caught up in the crowds demonstrating their gratitude at the expulsion of Glubb. Under-age most of them (little kids with sticks in their hands), they learn early how to become a mob—hooligans, people from the slums—busloads of them—streets full of gunfire—even late at night they haven't stopped; ("ooh ooh ooh," cry the women) all dishevelled—the other ambassadors can't even get about—only the ancient theater, completely empty, made an impression on me—like a photographic negative.

Tuesday, 2 July (in the air en route to Baghdad)

I set out with no great enthusiasm for this last farewell visit to Iraq. We took off shortly before 9, not at 8 according to the timetable. The delay is costing me; I was counting on my morning. The only book I've

1956

brought with me is the *Letters of Gertrude Bell*. They're only excerpts from the letters; who knows how much her family might have excised? I'm reading the letters from Baghdad, beginning in 1917. I read: "The days melt like snow in the sun"* (3.5.'17)—the works of man. "The great pleasure in this country is that I do love the people so much" (26.5.'17). I've often wondered what there may be to love about those peoples among whom I've been posted to serve for the last three and a half years. I haven't found it: self-interest, self-interest and baksheesh. Anything to take your mind a little higher, some sort of taste or style—that I haven't found. Perhaps Bell and Lawrence met different sorts of people, other classes that I haven't encountered, perhaps it's my fault for not knowing the language. But among the higher classes, the governing class that I *have* got to know—not a hint of nobility—only fanaticism and petulance—no generosity of spirit. But this bourgeoisie is a new phenomenon, unknown to those who helped it to rise to prominence—the sort of people who think they've reached the heights of civilization in buying a Cadillac or a gold-plated chandelier from Central Europe. What happens to a Bedouin tribal chief when you feed him for several months on Coca-Cola and give him a few cubic meters of concrete to live in? That's the question.

Our civilization has made a mire for them, which most probably was never foreseen by Lawrence or Bell.

Lebanese mountain villages, Anti-Lebanon, Damascus. Clearly from the air you can see that it's an *oasis*, and then immediately the desert begins again, black at first, then yellow, all dry watercourses like ribbons thrown down in disorder—suddenly the river.

Baghdad. But we're not descending. The whole city is shrouded in cloud. A sand-storm. Impossible to land in these conditions, the airplane heads for Tehran. And then on the return? Nobody can say. Maybe we'll be able to land at Baghdad. And if not, we'll land back at Beirut. So I'll have made this whole journey to no purpose—a whole day in an airplane. I go on with Gertrude Bell. She talks about the heat of July; 10th–20th of the month 122–122.8°—that's more than 50° centigrade. A friend observes to her that 115 is the limit of human tolerance. She speaks also about the burning wind, the very one we've left behind, beneath us.

Over Persia: mountains—saw-shaped peaks—rose-pink rock, a beautiful rose-pink. Here and there, in a watercourse, a touch of green and a few houses.

Gertrude: "The roses in my garden will be out in a week or two"—(1.3.'18). Here I am, travelling for nothing to the gardens of Isfahan.

1956

13:00 (Beirut time). We landed at Tehran. The frontier police, descendants of Xerxes' Great Army, behaved as though they were intent on making me pay for the deeds of Alexander the Great. A lowly cog in the wheels of order, with a bayonet (from another era) suspended from a belt that he couldn't tighten enough round his waist, pushed me, together with 7-8 unsought fellow-travellers, into the airfield buffet, having taken my passport—he seemed annoyed at the anomaly of our presence. The buffet is a very small room with space for only four round tables with nylon table-cloths. From the ceiling hang two large fans whose empty arms turn lazily, and two brass chandeliers in provocatively Art Nouveau style. I sat down at one of the middle tables with two typical Americans who were also bound for Baghdad. They've no idea, no interest in anything—they've resigned themselves patiently to this adventure, like a phenomenon of nature, reading thrillers. The heat is not very great. But there's no hope of getting out of this lazaretto. It's filled with a motley crowd, I'd have said of peasants in their Sunday best, people you wouldn't normally expect to see at an airfield. Sympathetic faces. The men remind you of Albanian-speakers in Greece. (I'm suddenly reminded that Persians are Aryans.) Some of the men are colossal, others terribly thin. Small children run between their legs. The women remind you of Persian miniatures—heavily made-up, almond eyes, some wearing American brassieres; most have colored kerchiefs (European) on their heads, and a tendency to pot-bellies caused by the tightness of the waistband. Suddenly, in the midst of this crowd, comes another of the same, one of the thin ones, with a bunch of flowers in his hand. He searched for a while, I imagine for the recipient of the bouquet, and disappeared. It was as though he'd given a signal. Little by little the room emptied. Only three women were left. One of them was pregnant, in a black-and-white checked blouse, fanning herself with a black fan that had a red pattern; the other was fat, in a dress the color of blackberry ice-cream, pink sandal-shoes with very high heels and a handbag of the same color; the third had large black eyes and the American brassiere. What happens to the ancient tribes when you feed them for a few years systematically on Coca-Cola and the rest of the baggage? This bastardization, something that we can't imagine even in Greece (where the same things are happening, and it's getting worse), is the thing that has disturbed me the most in these three and a half years that I've been living in these countries.

1956

The boredom of waiting begins. On my left is a large window. Through it I can see the airfield with parked aircraft like winged creatures asleep, and in the distance a line of mountains forming the horizon, with snow still on them. On my right the bar, with a huge intimidating *frigidaire*. In front of me the plate-glass window that separates us from the customs officials and the police, and at my back a long wooden couch. All the other furniture is made of nickel.

Gertrude: She was awakened, she says, one hour before dawn by the cannonade for Ramadan, to see the fire on which her gardener was roasting the last food they'd be permitted to eat, once it was light enough to distinguish a white thread from a black (22.6.'17).

15:00.—Enter three veiled women. Covered from top to toe, faces too, in black silk; very slim, as though someone had thrown a table-cloth over a pole. From the chinks of the material you could occasionally glimpse faces terribly pale, a world of difference from the three women I mentioned before and who are still here. With them is a man in a panama hat, an unkempt pepper-and-salt beard, with the eyes of a prophet.

Now the place has filled up with tarts—varnished nails, just like the first three. Behind me some tall gawky youths took off their shoes and sat down cross-legged on the wooden couch. In front of me the whole bevy of females huddled by the window to stare out. Behind them stood a venerable Hodja, priestly in appearance.

Time passed, somehow. We started out at 16:30 (Beirut time). The pilot is in a bad temper. I ask him, as he passes, on his way to the aircraft, what news from Baghdad?

"None," he replies, in English.

I'm determined to try. If we can't land this time, I'll simply sleep in my bed in Beirut and have had a journey into Persia for nothing. The airplane is full to bursting with pilgrims bound for Mecca (they change planes at Beirut, for Jedda). They carry with them every imaginable thing. Baskets, bric-a-brac, bundles. With them are the three veiled women and the Hodja, who as we're sitting down to fasten our seatbelts wants to find the toilet.

Gertrude: To an old servant of hers in Aleppo: "Oh Fattuh, before the war our hearts were so light when we travelled, now they are so heavy that a camel could not carry us" (17.10.'19). Not to mention an airplane!

Gertrude: "And this country, which way will it go with all these 'agents of unrest' to tempt it?" (4.1.'20). Thirty-six years have passed and the "agents of unrest" are as active as ever; sometimes, it's true, like a cat licking cream off a knife.

1956

An hour and a half later, we were again over Baghdad:

"The weather has improved," the co-pilot informs me. "We'll begin our descent and take it from there."

We made our descent and landed. Waiting for me at the airfield, as well as our own staff, was a representative of the Iraqi Foreign Ministry and the Italian ambassador, Lanza. I ate at his embassy in the evening. He's fascinated by British policy, the Iraqi prime minister Nuri Said, and the Turks. Long talk about Cyprus. I don't know if I managed to get out of his head the persistent idea that resistance to British rule there is the work of Communists. He's writing something about Gertrude Bell, who he says was responsible for the idea of installing King Faisal in Baghdad. He says she committed suicide.

Tuesday, 3 July

Farewell round of visits. Luckily, the king received me at once (*faveur spéciale*, the master of ceremonies, Tahsin Qadri, told me). Heat around 47 °C, but the room is reasonably cool. Slept well.

From my window the Tigris and on the far bank palm-trees. For me there's something graceful about this great river—also the great gardens with their date-palms.

I find in Iraq a more integrated character than in the other countries where I serve.

Gertrude: "One woman" (Armenian, a refugee) "when she first saw the Tigris burst into tears. 'Ah,' she cried, 'the mass of water here! And my sister died in the desert of thirst'" (29.12.'17).

I remember the wooden votive offerings with candles, on the way down to the water's edge.

Of course Great Britain is doing all she can to hold on to her oil-wells (*this* is where her real efforts ought to lie, not in Cyprus over bases that are already lost to her); now she's got the Baghdad Accord, which is above all a British affair. She's running it (at the airfield yesterday I met Lord Jellicoe, son of the admiral, who's working in the organization for the Accord). But the American Embassy has twice the personnel of the British, and the first university in Iraq is being organized by American Jesuits. The Accord depends on Prime Minister Nuri, who is old and sick, and on the small class of sheikhs who stick with the British so as not to lose their wealth. Below those, the bourgeoisie that's in the ascendant loathes Britain.

Gertrude: "If we leave this country to go to the dogs, it will mean that we shall have to reconsider our whole position in Asia. If Mesopotamia goes Persia goes

1956

inevitably, and then India. And the place which we leave empty will be occupied by seven devils a good deal worse than any which existed before we came" (10.4.'20). But now that India has gone? And Persia too?

I remember one night Rex Leeper at his embassy,* just after the war, at a difficult moment during the regency—speaking in the same tone about Greece: "If we leave this country to go to the dogs . . ."

Now, with their mania for sucking up to the Turks over Cyprus, they've alienated even Greece—God help us.

Gertrude: "What a dreadful world of broken friendships we have created between us" (16.1.'18).

How many Englishmen who have known Greece must be thinking the same thing now, after the indescribable damage done by Eden?

Gertrude: "It would be an unthinkable crime to abandon those who have loyally served us" (8.2.'18).

But they did, and there's no hope they won't go on doing it. It's strange, the Englishman thinks nothing of the hatred he arouses around him—only, now, he doesn't have many options left.

Wednesday, 4 July (in the air en route to Damascus)

At the airfield, the heat was so great, I felt myself begin to wilt. A cup of tea improved matters.

Gertrude: "Alexander, who died there" (in Babylon) "in the palace on the northern mound" 18.4.'18 (must check). Alexander the Great, I have him all the time on my mind. Marching his army through this furnace with all that Macedonian ironmongery on their backs.

Sunday evening, 8 July. Beirut

We got back here on Friday morning. This morning I tried to write something. Amazing how heavy this climate makes you feel. I think I'd prefer the fiery heat of Baghdad. I'm glad to be leaving all this. Enough.

All the same, I'd like to have a little time in Athens, a little time for writing. I've been away from my country since January '48.

Wednesday, 11 July. Amman

As I go about on my various visits I try to take some photographs from the car (a long-range taxi), scenes of the road.

"Watch out," the driver says to me. He's a Palestinian refugee (Basil is his name). "It's forbidden. If the police see you, they'll make trouble."

"Why?"

"The police say the Americans take photos of them and publish them in America. The photos show them up as poor and uncivilized—they aren't like us Palestinians, you know."

I'm glad to be leaving behind these attitudes—these chaotic minds mired in complexes, for whom nothing is what it seems.

One of the reasons that the Christian Arabs don't get on with the Orthodox Patriarchate, apart from the main one (they want to get their hands on its wealth, which they suppose to be legendary), is this feeling that the monks regard them as uncivilized and uneducated, even if they're people of some learning. Even educated Christians among the Arabs complain the Orthodox hierarchy treats them like barbarians. It's just like the Americans taking photographs.

Thursday, 12 July. Jerusalem

We arrived yesterday evening at 18:15. A different climate here, more human; it's as if you've been travelling on another planet (I include Beirut here);

a light coolness, scented air that opens up the heart. The only place I'll regret, now that I'm leaving, is this place of refuge we've found in Jerusalem, the "American Colony." As we were coming by car—perhaps because of the time of year—I remembered the first time I'd come to Jerusalem in '42, thanks to Rommel—fourteen years ago. It feels like yesterday. I wasn't very young then—and now I don't feel as though I've aged.

NOTES

p. xiii, English translation: A Poet's Journal: Days of 1945–1951, translated by Athan Anagnostopoulos, with an introduction by Walter Kaiser (Harvard University Press, 1974). On the subject of GS as diarist there is an unpublished Ph.D. thesis in French by Vassiliki Contoyanni; at King's College London, Nikolaos Falagkas is currently completing a doctoral dissertation on the "Greek private diary," which will include close readings of the diaries of Seferis. The standard English translation of Seferis's complete poetry is *George Seferis: Collected Poems*, translated, edited, and introduced by Edmund Keeley and Philip Sherrard (Princeton University Press, Revised Edition, 1995). His selected essays can be found in *On the Greek Style: Selected Essays in Poetry and Hellenism*, translated by Rex Warner and Th. Frangopoulos (Atlantic/Little Brown, 1966).

p. xix, a Greek world: Entry for November 6, 1953.

p. 9, Why, you'll see your children: Maro Seferis had been obliged to leave behind in occupied Greece her two young daughters, by her previous marriage, in order to follow her husband.

p. 12, when the German attack began: The Battle of Crete had begun two days earlier, with German parachutists taking the airfield of Maleme outside Chania, then the capital of the island.

p. 13, Nanis ... and Timos: Nanis Panagiotopoulos (to whom the poem "An Old Man on the River-Bank" would be dedicated the following year—see p. 19) and Timos Malanos, both businessmen and amateur men of letters who belonged to the settled Greek community of Alexandria. Both would become firm friends of GS and Maro during their time in Egypt. Malanos is today regarded as an important literary critic, the first to devote a book to the poetry of Cavafy. Malanos's later critical work on the poetry of GS would lead to a total rupture between the two men.

p. 14, ancient Helleno-Syrian magi: GS quotes from the poem "According to the Recipes of Helleno-Syrian Magi" by Cavafy (my translation), which invokes the culturally mixed world of Alexandria under the Roman Empire in a plaintive lament for aging.

p. 14, "entering the whirlpool": An allusion to Part IV of T.S. Eliot's "The Waste Land."

p. 15, the crowd of people I serve: GS refers principally here to the politicians who made up the Greek government-in-exile—along with whom he had been displaced first from Athens, then from Crete—but also to his senior colleagues in the Greek civil service.

p. 15, Hypatia: This happened in 415 C.E. The mob was Christian and its victim a pagan female mathematician and philosopher.

p. 15, Nikolaidis ... Palairet: Nikos Nikolaidis (1884-1956): Greek-Cypriot writer, principally of short stories and novels, who from 1923 until his death lived in Cairo, regarded today as one of the major Cypriot authors of the period; also a playwright and painter. Some of his work has been published in a bilingual edition in English (ed. Maria Roussou: Diaspora Books, 1998). Elli Papadimitriou, a childhood friend of GS, was at this time a committed Communist and writer; later she would edit a ground-breaking anthology of Greek oral history. Sir Michael Palairet had been the last British ambassador to Greece before the German invasion.

p. 15, once she knew we were leaving: GS had just learned that he was about to be transferred to the Greek Embassy in Pretoria, South Africa.

p. 15, Tsouderos: Emmanuel Tsouderos, prime minister throughout most of the period when the legitimate Greek government was in exile (1941–44).

p. 15, Chareh el Wabour Faransaoui: Here GS gives the Arabic street-name transliterated into French—his first foreign language—perhaps because he was struck by the transformation of the familiar French words: *vapeur* and *français*.

p. 16, imprinting ... waxed paper: GS was fascinated, all through his period of exile in Egypt, by the possibilities for reproducing a book of poems in manuscript, as a kind of handicraft, or throw-back to the days before printing, in defiance of conventional printing methods. His own next book of poems, *Logbook II*, published in Alexandria in 1944, would take this form, though by a different process from that described here.

p. 18, "Days of June '41": The dateline is part of the original poem, the opening one in the collection *Logbook II*. The references to the new moon "holding the old one in her arms" allude to the traditional Scottish ballad "Sir Patrick Spens," in which the image is a presage of disaster to come. The "beautiful island bloodied" is Crete, overrun by German paratroopers between May 20 and 30, 1941.

p. 19, "An Old Man ...": The dateline places this poem near the end of the silence, lasting several months, in GS's diary that would be broken by the entry for June 26. The impending crisis described in that and the following entry forms part of the implicit background to the poem. The first and fifth lines, it has been suggested by Christopher Williams in an unpublished University of London Ph.D. thesis (1996), may have been intended as a reply to Churchill's famous statement of this time: "Let us go forward together." Alternatively, or additionally, they could be read as a response to T.S. Eliot, "The Dry Salvages" III (published 1941): "And do not think of the fruit of the action. / Fare forward ... / Not fare well, / But fare forward, voyagers."

p. 23, Larry: Lawrence Durrell, at this time foreign press officer in the Publicity Section of the British Embassy in Cairo, in effect responsible for propaganda.

p. 23, Kanellopoulos: Panagiotis Kanellopoulos, deputy prime minister and minister for defense in the exiled Greek government.

p. 23, heir to the throne: Crown Prince (later King) Paul, brother of King George II of the Hellenes, who at this time exercised his role as head of the Greek state from London. GS had always a marked antipathy towards the Greek monarchy.

p. 24, the army: The Free Greek army, a force of two brigades, consisting of volunteers who had escaped from occupied Greece.

p. 24, back to South Africa: GS had already spent nine months at the Greek Embassy in Pretoria, from August 1941 to April 1942.

p. 24, the consulate in Alexandria: Center of a large Greek-speaking population that had been established in the city since the early nineteenth century, and in its heyday had included the poet Cavafy.

p. 33, Albania: Reference to the Albanian front, where Greek troops beat back superior invading forces from Fascist Italy between October 1940 and early April 1941.

p. 37, Papadimitriou: See p. 154, note *p. 15, Nikolaidis ... Palairet.*

p. 39, I've started writing something: This refers to the poem "Stratis Thalassinos at the Dead Sea," p. 45.

p. 41, Mount Athos: Athos, the Holy Mountain of Orthodoxy, a monastic republic in the north of Greece, to which entry is forbidden to women. It boasts more than thirty functioning monasteries, the oldest dating back to the tenth century. See also the poem "Stratis Thalassinos at the Dead Sea," p. 45.

p. 42, the sacrament of baptism: In the Greek Orthodox tradition the pilgrimage to the Holy Land, culminating in a second baptism in the waters of the Jordan, is the equivalent of the Hajj for Muslims. In former times someone who had completed this pilgrimage would have the prefix "Hadji-" added to his name.

p. 42, Megara: Town in Greece, on the road between Athens and Corinth.

p. 42, Franks: Historically, the word in Greek refers to western Europeans; in context here it designates primarily Roman Catholics.

p. 45, Stratis Thalassinos: The name Stratis Thalassinos (Wayfarer the Seafarer) first appears as a poetic persona or alter ego in writings of Seferis from his time in London in the early 1930s.

p. 45, THIS IS THE PLACE GENTLEMEN: The words in capitals appear in English in the original.

p. 52, the Ministry of War: The ministry of the exiled Greek government, housed at the time in Cairo. For Kanellopoulos see p. 156, note *p. 23 Kanellopoulos*.

p. 53, 1821: Date of the outbreak of the Greek War of Independence against the Ottoman Empire; by extension the date itself has come to denote that conflict.

p. 54, Synesios: Synesios (370–413 C.E.): bishop of Ptolemaïs in Libya, a Neoplatonist philosopher and pupil of Hypatia (see p.154, note *p. 15, Hypatia*). Heraclius: the last Byzantine emperor to conquer territories in what is now the Middle East, before the Arab invasions of the 640s C.E.

p. 54, Not by stones ... wheresoe'er they be: Paraphrase or pastiche by Aelius Aristeides (117–189 C.E.), an orator associated with GS's native city of Smyrna, of a lost poem by the sixth-century B.C.E. lyric poet Alcaeus. GS quotes the original Ancient Greek.

p. 55, To meet a distinguished person: This sentence in English in the original.

p. 57, Timos: Malanos. See p. 153, note *p. 13 Nanis ... and Timos*.

p. 57, just such a severed head: The concluding lines of Cavafy's poem, which refers to the murder of the Roman general Pompey in 48 B.C.E. in Alexandria. Theodotos was the flunky sent to convey to the victorious Julius Caesar the head of his arch-rival. Caesar reacted with disgust.

p. 58, my father: Stelios Seferiades (1873–1951), a successful international lawyer and academic, had in his younger days published poems and literary translations in the periodical press of Smyrna. The anecdote gives a hint of the troubled relationship between father and son, neither of whom seems to have had much time for the poetic aspirations of the other.

p. 59, this is my first autumn: The months between September 1941 and April 1942 Seferis had spent in the southern hemisphere, in South Africa.

p. 61, the Seventh: Symphony by Beethoven, presumably.

p. 62, Sharia Emad-el-Din: Street in central Cairo where the offices of the Greek government-in-exile were situated. Soon GS and Maro would move into their own rented apartment on this same street.

p. 64, Buckley's: Christopher Buckley, correspondent for the *Times* of London.

p. 64, Bairam: Greek name (from Turkish) for the Muslim festival of Eid al-Adha.

p. 64, Fierce fighting continues: In this laconic way GS records the first news of the decisive Second Battle of El Alamein.

p. 66, Leland Stowe: One of the foreign war correspondents that GS had come to know while acting as spokesman for the foreign press in Athens during the winter of 1940-41.

p. 67, Skala: Village on the coast near GS's birthplace of Smyrna/Izmir, where he spent his childhood summers, and which he would long after remember as "the only place that, even now, I can call home in the most rooted sense of the word" (written in 1941).

p. 70, behind the lines that Cairo had become: Since the Second Battle of El Alamein in October 1942, in which Free Greek troops played a small but distinguished part, the war front had moved far to the west of Cairo.

p. 73, Trial of the Accents: Yannis Kakrides, a professor of Classics at the University of Athens and future translator, with Nikos Kazantzakis, of the *Iliad* and the *Odyssey* into Modern Greek, was arraigned during winter and spring of 1941-42, while Greeks in their thousands were dying of starvation in the streets of Athens, for the offense of publishing an academic article in the spoken, or "demotic," form of Greek, instead of the officially sanctioned *katharevousa*, and without the traditional accent-marks that had first been used in the third century B.C.E.

p. 73, Larry and Nancy: Lawrence Durrell and his first wife.

p. 74, Ramón Gómez de la Serna: Flamboyant and prolific Spanish avant-garde writer, sometimes considered an early surrealist (1891-1963).

p. 74, Katsimbalis: George Katsimbalis (1897-1979), close friend of GS, immortalized by Henry Miller as the "Colossus of Maroussi."

p. 74, "Mythology II": Lawrence Durrell, *Collected Poems 1931-1974*, Faber, p. 115. The poetic "traffic" or "circulation" mentioned here would continue in the work of Durrell, with Bernard Spencer and

Nanos Valaoritis, to produce the first book of translations of GS's own poetry into English, in 1948. It may have been this that GS had in mind when he contributed his "ideas about poems," under the transparent pseudonym of Mathaios Pascal, to the periodical *Personal Landscape* (vol. 2, part 3, 1944), which appeared in Cairo under the editorship of Durrell and Spencer. This is GS writing in English:

"All poems written or unwritten exist. I don't mean a Platonic but a biological existence. Their relation to their written form is the relation of the model to its portrait. The special ability of the poet is to see them: that's why the poets are sometimes called seers.

"The faculty of seeing them makes the poet, the faculty of painting (i.e., writing) them makes the talent of the poet. That's why we may have (and had) poets without talent; but mere talent without the poetical gift (i.e., the gift of the seer) is inconceivable.

"Poems do not live alone...."

p. 74, *Karaghiozis*: Durrell's reported words in the following paragraphs are given in English. I have added missing punctuation to the sentence that begins "First-rate." In the Greek translation of the poem that immediately follows, "Marmion" is rendered as "the great Karaghiozis." Karaghiozis is the comical trickster anti-hero of the traditional Greek shadow-puppet show which takes his name.

p. 75, *Palamas*: Kostis Palamas (1859–1943), who had recently died in occupied Athens, was a prolific poet who had dominated the Athenian literary scene for five decades.

p. 77, *"The King of Asine"*: Poem by GS completed and published in 1940, which includes the lines "a void always with us" and "The poet is a void." The same poem also speaks of "the weight / the nostalgia for the weight of a living existence."

p. 78, *André Gide*: Gide was at this time living in Tunis, now liberated by the Allies. GS had met him in Athens shortly before the outbreak of war.

p. 79, Henri al-Kayem: Leading Alexandrian intellectual from the 1930s until 1960, who wrote in French and was admired by poets of the stature of Pierre Jean Jouve (mentioned here, some of whose poems GS had translated into Greek) and René Char. Much of his work was published in Paris.

p. 81, "Mountebanks, Middle East": The verse form of the translation follows that of the original closely.

p. 83, river-bank: See the poem, "An Old Man on the River-Bank", pp. 19–21.

p. 85, "The Dry Salvages": T.S. Eliot's poem, the third of the *Four Quartets*. Xydis: see p. 163, note *p. 106, Alekos Xydis*.

p. 85, Canzona: "Canzona di ringraziamento" (Song of Thanksgiving), Beethoven's title for the slow movement of his string quartet op. 132, an especial favorite of GS. In 1948 Seferis would adopt this title for a poem of his own.

p. 85, Peristeria: Exclusive meeting-place for Europeans that overlooks the Nile. The name is Greek, and means "pigeons" or "doves."

p. 85, Kingfisher: The last word appears in English in the original.

p. 85, I've resigned ... Press: GS had been the official spokesman of the Greek government-in-exile since the summer of 1942. In the wake of the failed mutinies of the Greek armed forces stationed in Egypt in April 1944, the exiled government was drastically overhauled. A short time later, GS was forced to resign from his job.

p. 87, John of the Cross: Sixteenth-century Spanish mystic poet, author of "Noche del Espiritu" ("The Dark Night of the Soul"). GS first encountered this work in 1931 and attached great importance to the following passage from the commentary by Jean Baruzi (II.1): "He who learns the finest 'particularities' of a vocation or an art 'goes always in darkness,' rather than [letting himself be guided] by his original knowledge, because, if he did not leave [that knowledge] behind him, he would never reach the point of liberating himself from it."

p. 87, Timos: Malanos, see p. 153, note *p. 13, Nanis ... and Timos* and p. 162, note *p. 90.*

p. 87, Sweeney ... bamboo: Eliot's *Sweeney Agonistes: Fragments of an Aristophanic Melodrama.* GS quotes (in English) the first line of the "Song by Wauchope and Horsfall."

p. 87, This aestheticism of the ivory tower: A highly condensed and one-sided account of a major literary quarrel between the two friends, conducted through several letters of April and May 1944, in the course of which GS had written to Malanos: "Literature is not, by its very nature, something that can exist 'happily' or 'unhappily.' Art is not the great forgetting; art is the great consciousness, and it isn't a consolation, it's a torment, it's a struggle.... Art for me is something out there and I serve it, because I cannot do otherwise."

p. 87, these last few months: GS blamed British policy and interference for the collapse of morale in the Greek armed forces in Egypt and the resulting mutiny. He was also bitterly critical of the measures taken by the British to quell the uprising and punish the mutineers.

p. 88, the first batch to Greece: With the German withdrawal from Greece imminent, GS at this point expected that he would be transferred directly to Athens upon the liberation.

p. 90, Timos: Malanos would see GS's next collection of poems, *Logbook II*, through press shortly after their departure from Egypt.

p. 92, Nanis, Timos: See p. 153, note *p. 13, Nanis ... and Timos* and p. 162, note *p. 90.*

p. 93, Alexandria is leaving: A reference to the poem by Cavafy, "The God Abandons Antony": "Say farewell to her, the Alexandria that is leaving."

p. 93, Cor Scorpionis: Latin: "the heart of Scorpio." The same phrase, translated into Greek, would appear in GS's poem *"Thrush"* written two years later.

p. 94, "Last Stop": This poem was written too late to be included in the first edition of *Logbook II*, which came out at about the same time in Alexandria. It was added to the second edition, which appeared in Athens just over a year later; in that and all subsequent editions it occupies the final position in the collection. The italicized phrase, *pain-perpetuating memory of pain* is my rendering of the phrase in Ancient Greek, *mnesimemon ponos*, which Seferis takes directly from Aeschylus' *Agamemnon*. This translation was first published, in an earlier version, in the journal *Arion* (vol. 13, no. 2, 2005).

p. 102, Acropolis ... English translation: *Six Nights on the Acropolis*, translated by Susan Matthias (River Vale, NJ: Cosmos Publishing <www.greeceinprint.com>, 2007).

p. 104, There is no landlord: This whole entry is in English in the original. "H4" identifies a refuelling stop along the oil pipeline from Baghdad. There are only a handful of entries for 1953 before GS's visit to Cyprus, except for those associated with his visit to the grave of Ianthe (see below).

p. 104, Ianthe: Greek pseudonym adopted by Jane Digby (1807–1881), an English society lady who married an Arab sheikh and lived for many years on the edge of the desert, near Damascus.

p. 106, Alekos Xydis: A younger colleague in the diplomatic service and a friend.

p. 106, "Here was inspired ... Barrès": In French in the original. For Barrès, see p. 168, note *p. 130, Renan*.

p. 107, Cavafy's perfumed youths: Allusion to the poem by C.P. Cavafy, "Young Men of Sidon (400 A.D.)."

p. 107, Hester Stanhope: Another society lady (1776-1839) from Britain, who made an unorthodox life for herself and died in these parts. The village of Djoun had been given to her by the local ruler as a personal fief.

p. 107, Melchites–Uniates: That is, Orthodox Christians who accept the abortive union of the Orthodox and Catholic churches concluded in 1439 but repudiated shortly afterwards by the mainstream Orthodox Church.

p. 107, So you seek the sorceress of Djoun: This sentence and the first words of the speech that follows are in French in the original.

p. 109, missions such as mine: GS was simultaneously ambassador to four countries: Lebanon, Syria, Jordan, and Iraq.

p. 110, coca-cola-ism, pepsi-cola-ism: GS's coinages in Greek.

p. 110, Pelecanus onocrotalus: See p. 10, entry for May 19, 1941.

p. 110, frigidaire: in Roman characters in GS's journal.

p. 112, I begin to think: The whole of this entry in English in the original.

p. 113, like Corfu, like Salonica: Places with a formerly distinct cultural identity, assimilated into the Greek state after 1864 and 1912, respectively.

p. 113, Evangelos Louizos and Maurice Cardiff: Louizos was a Cypriot lawyer, at whose house outside Famagusta GS and Maro would stay on subsequent visits to Cyprus. Cardiff, at the time British Council Representative in Nicosia, had become a friend during an earlier posting to Athens at the end of World War II. Given the political sensitivities of the time, it was important to GS to emphasize the private nature of this first visit to Cyprus.

p. 114, the Ethnarch: Archbishop Makarios III, who would soon emerge as the political leader of the Greek Cypriot struggle for union with Greece (*Enosis*) and would become the first president of the independent Republic of Cyprus from its establishment in 1960 until his death in 1977. By a tradition dating back to Ottoman rule in Cyprus, the spiritual leader of the Orthodox Church had the title of "Ethnarch" or "leader of the nation," a role that carried expectations of secular as well as religious leadership. This was GS's first meeting with Makarios, for whom over the next six years he would develop a profound admiration.

p. 116, Agianapa ... sycamore-tree: The ruined Venetian monastery of Agia Napa, in the south-east corner of Cyprus, where GS saw this tree and was photographed standing underneath it, is today almost lost among the brash new buildings of the tourist resort that has sprung up since the 1980s. The line of verse would be developed later into the first line of the published poem "Agianapa II."

p. 117, "Engomi": Many details of this entry are taken up in the poem "Engomi," which would be published in 1955. The lines that follow in the diary represent GS's earliest draft of the later poem.

p. 117, tekke: Sufi chapel in the Turkish quarter of Nicosia, by the Kyrenia Gate. This entry is one of relatively few in which GS directs his attention to the Turkish-speaking Muslim minority of Cyprus. Until 1963, the Greek Cypriot and Turkish Cypriot communities were not formally separated. The present-day division of the island dates from 1974.

p. 118, Mustafa Kemal Pasha: The founder and first president of the Turkish Republic, better known by the name he adopted towards the end of his life: Atatürk, meaning "father of the Turks."

p. 119, 11 January, Beirut: In the published Greek text this entry appears under the date "Monday, 7 January 1952." But on that date GS was in London and there is no other evidence that he was interested in revising his novel at that time. I believe that the entry has been misdated; the dateline that appears in the main text is my own emendation. The style of this entry is unusually "unfinished" for GS, seemingly recording almost the stream of consciousness of a moment, and never revised or "written up."

p. 119, copying out the Acropolis: The first sketches for the novel *Six Nights on the Acropolis* had been made in Athens during the years mentioned; GS appears to have transposed material from his own diary to that of his fictional hero and vice versa, during the process of rewriting referred to here.

p. 119, La guerre nous mange le sexe: "The war is eating up our sex lives." Compare the entries in Part I, passim.

p. 120, Venizelos: Eleftherios Venizelos (1861-1936), Greek statesman who dominated the political life of the country for more than three decades; one of the few political figures admired by Seferis almost without reservation.

p. 121, Driving power–tremendous: This phrase in English in the original.

p. 121, Lady Hester Stanhope: See p. 164, note *p. 107, Hester Stanhope.*

p. 121, 1839: In English in the original.

p. 121, environs of Sidon: GS's expression no doubt deliberately conflates the titles of two poems by Cavafy, "In the Environs of Antioch" (usually translated as "On the Outskirts ...") and "Young Men of Sidon (400 A.D.)," and also of two of his own that he was writing at this time: "In the Environs of Kyrenia" ("In the Kyrenia District" is the standard English translation) and "Peddler from Sidon."

p. 122, Friday 16 April, Amman: The few diary entries for 1954 up to and including this one are given in their entirety. As in the preceding year, GS is extremely sparing in his diary coverage, except for his experience of the Orthodox Easter celebrations in Jerusalem and his visit to Cyprus later in the year.

p. 122, famous map: Mosaic map of Jerusalem that dates from the sixth century C.E.

p. 123, talanto: Sounding-block (*semantron*): a block of wood struck with a baton, in the Orthodox church often replacing bells. The word *talanto*, in the Orthodox tradition, can also be used for this, but here GS refers to a specific rhythm of striking the sounding-block, associated with the monasteries of Mount Athos (see p. 156, note *p. 41, Mount Athos*).

p. 123, Apo-o-o-o-ollo: The cry of the doomed priestess Cassandra in *Agamemnon*, Aeschylus' tragedy of the fifth century B.C.E.

p. 124, in a dry and thirsty land, where no water is: GS quotes Psalm 63:1 in the Greek of the Septuagint. The translation is taken from the 1610 King James Version.

p. 128, "Erotikos logos": Poem included in GS's first collection, *Turning Point* (1931), written in Athens in 1929–30.

p. 129, "monster": Details from this entry, as from that of November 13, 1953, would shortly find their way into the poem "Engomi," translated on pp. 133–35.

p. 129, Despina and Anna: GS's niece Despina Tsatsou; Anna Londou, daughter of GS's wife by her first marriage.

p. 129, Renan: see below.

p. 130, Renan: Ernest Renan (1823–92) was best known in his lifetime for his secularizing *Life of Jesus* (1861). In the 1860s he lived, with his sister Henriette, in the village visited by GS, where he conducted archaeological excavations. He is perhaps best remembered today for his work on the politics of nationalism. Maurice Barrès (1862–1923): French writer and politician of extreme nationalist opinions, whose work, including a book on GS's compatriot El Greco, GS seems not to have liked.

p. 130, when the camera is properly adjusted: This is how the diary for 1954 ends.

p. 132, Bhamdoun: Summer resort in the hills above Beirut, where most of the poems of *Logbook III* were written. All the poems mentioned in this entry form part of that collection, which first appeared in Athens on the last day of 1955 with the title, . . . *Cyprus, Where It Was Ordained For Me* . . . The poem "Engomi" has the final place in the collection.

p. 136, Glubb Pasha: Sir John Bagot Glubb (1897–1986) was General of the Arab Legion in Transjordan and since the Second World War had become the effective ruler of the Kingdom of Jordan. A fluent speaker of Arabic, he wore Arab dress in public. His downfall in March 1956 was one of the factors that led to the Suez Crisis later in the year.

p. 136, Coghill: Brigadier Coghill, expelled from Jordan along with Glubb Pasha, was the brother of Neville Coghill, who translated Chaucer's *Canterbury Tales* into Modern English, and whom GS would have known from his eighteen-month posting to London in 1951–52.

p. 136, "British have been taken by surprise": In English in the original.

p. 137, "Rain is not good for politics": In English in the original.

p. 137, Freya Stark [and Perowne]: GS refers to her only as "the writer," omitting her name. More famous than her husband, the colonial administrator Stewart Perowne, Freya Stark had written extensively about her travels in the Middle East.

p. 138, "The days ... sun": Direct quotations from these letters, in this and subsequent entries, are in English in the original.

p. 146, Leeper at his embassy: Leeper had been British ambassador to Greece during the period (1945–46) when GS was political secretary to the regent, Archbishop Damaskinos. See also p. 99.

PHOTOS AND ILLUSTRATIONS

Frontispiece: Title page in GS's handwriting added to the original pages covering the dates indicated. The first word underlined means "diary," the large heading "Beirut" (in red ink in the original), and below it "Cyprus" with the corresponding dates of GS's visit, and below it his signature. Most of his diaries were originally written on these small loose sheets of squared paper. Reproduced from *Meres 6*, ed. Panagiotis Mermigkas (Ikaros, 1986), p. 65.

p. v: From *Logbook II*, autograph copy, p. 8. Reproduced from the first, calligraphic edition (Alexandria, 1944). All drawings from the volume appear courtesy of the Rare Books Division, Department of Rare Books and Special Collections, Princeton University Library. The date (11 September 1941) is the actual date of writing for the poem that appears on p. 18. The drawing is a schematic representation of Alexandria, showing the Gate of the Sun and the Gate of the Moon, mentioned in the poem, as well as on p. 15. Also shown are the Qait Bey fortress (mentioned on p. 76) and (probably) the direction of air raids.

p. vi: GS in Cairo, 1944. Reproduced from *Oi fotografies tou Giorgou Seferi* (Cultural Foundation of the National Bank [MIET], 2000), p. 63.

p. 11: From *Logbook II*, autograph copy, p. 16.

p. 49: From *Logbook II*, autograph copy, p. 28. First page of the poem "Stratis Thalassinos at the Dead Sea." The epigraph ends with the words, in brackets: "Letter of S[tratis] Th[alassinos] from Jerusalem," not included in later editions. On the left, a depth gauge shows the level of the Dead Sea in relation to that of the Aegean (written-in vertically, in capitals).

p. 62: From *Logbook II*, autograph copy, p. 22. The drawing of the desk, described in the diary, accompanies the poem "Crickets" (not translated in this volume) and includes the dateline of that poem: "Transvaal, 16 Jan. [19]42."

p. 82: First page of the poem "Mountebanks, Middle East," from *Logbook II*, autograph copy, p. 40.

p. 111: GS at Jerash, Jordan, October 1953. Reproduced from *Oi fotografies tou Giorgou Seferi*, p. 93.

p. 151: From *Logbook II*, autograph copy, p. 27. Compare the descriptions of palm-trees in the last line of the poem "An Old Man on the River-Bank" (p. 21) and on p. 88 (entry for 21 August 1944).

p. 173: GS at the home he shared with Maro in Beirut, on the rue Georges Picot (Cultural Foundation of the National Bank [MIET], photographic archive of George Seferis).

George Seferis was born in Smyrna in 1900 and moved with his family to Athens when he was fourteen. He was appointed to the Greek Ministry of Foreign Affairs in 1926 and subsequently served in Greece, England, and Albania, before accompanying the Greek government-in-exile to Crete, Egypt, and South Africa. He was stationed in Cairo from 1942–44, then served as ambassador to Lebanon, Syria, Jordan, and Iraq from 1953–56, and to England from 1957–62. His books of poems include Mythistorema *(1935),* "Thrush" *(1947), and* Logbook I, II, III *(1940, 1944, 1955). He was awarded the Nobel Prize for Literature in 1963 and died in Athens in 1971.*

OTHER BOOKS BY IBIS EDITIONS

BAGHDAD, YESTERDAY
THE MAKING OF AN ARAB JEW
by Sasson Somekh

SADDER THAN WATER:
NEW & SELECTED POEMS
by Samih al-Qasim
Translated by Nazih Kassis, introduced by Adina Hoffman

SARAYA, THE OGRE'S DAUGHTER
by Emile Habiby
Translated by Peter Theroux

IN SEARCH OF A LOST LADINO:
LETTER TO ANTONIO SAURA
by Marcel Cohen
Translated and introduced by Raphael Rubinstein

THE FULLNESS OF TIME:
POEMS BY GERSHOM SCHOLEM
Edited and introduced by Steven Wasserstrom
Translated by Richard Sieburth

THE COLLECTED POEMS
OF AVRAHAM BEN YITZHAK
Edited and with an afterword by Hannan Hever
Translated by Peter Cole

STATIONS OF DESIRE:
LOVE ELEGIES FROM IBN 'ARABI AND NEW POEMS
by Michael Sells

THISTLES: SELECTED POEMS OF ESTHER RAAB
Translated and introduced by Harold Schimmel

NEVER MIND: TWENTY POEMS AND A STORY
by Taha Muhammad Ali
Translated by Peter Cole, Yahya Hijazi, and Gabriel Levin

REVEALMENT AND CONCEALMENT: FIVE ESSAYS
by Haim Nahman Bialik
Afterword by Zali Gurevitch

THE LITTLE BOOKSELLER OUSTAZ ALI
by Ahmed Rassim
Translated by Gabriel Levin

QASIDA
by Harold Schimmel
Translated by Peter Cole

FROM ISLAND TO ISLAND
by Harold Schimmel
Translated by Peter Cole

ON THE SEA
by Yehuda Halevi
Translated by Gabriel Levin

COSTIGAN
by Dennis Silk

LIFE ISN'T ALL BIKE-CLIPS
by Dennis Silk

HEZEKIAH'S TUNNEL
by Gabriel Levin

Ibis Editions is a small press founded in Jerusalem in 1998 and dedicated to the publication of Levant-related books of poetry and prose. The press publishes translations from Hebrew, Arabic, French, and the other languages of the region. Ibis is a non-profit organization motivated by the belief that literary work, especially when translated into a common language, can serve as an important vehicle for the promotion of understanding between individuals and peoples, and for the discovery of common ground. For more information about the press, see www.ibiseditions.com.